D0397149

BUCCANEER HARBOR

ALSO BY PETER BRIGGS

Science Ship: A Voyage Aboard the *Discoverer*

Men in the Sea

Mysteries of Our World

Rivers in the Sea

The Great Global Rift

Water: The Vital Essence

BUCCANEER

THE FABULOUS HISTORY OF

HARBOR

PORT ROYAL, JAMAICA

by Peter Briggs

SIMON AND SCHUSTER · NEW YORK

WITHDRAWN

All rights reserved
including the right of reproduction
in whole or in part in any form
Copyright © 1970 by Peter Briggs
Published by Simon and Schuster, Children's Book Division
Rockefeller Center, 630 Fifth Avenue
New York, New York 10020

First Printing

SBN 671-65127—7 Trade
SBN 671-65126—9 Library ·
Library of Congress Catalog Card Number: 74-107272
Manufactured in the United States of America
By The Book Press Inc., Brattleboro, Vermont
Designed by Betty Crumley

I would particularly like to thank Mr. Philip Mayes of the Jamaica
National Trust, who is in charge of the restoration at Port Royal, and
Mr. C. Bernard Lewis, Director of the Institute of Jamaica in Kingston, for their assistance in the research on this book.

P.B.

17430

Contents

BUCCANEER HARBOR

At the Beginning

Here is the tale of a city, one that during its brief life span became the richest and most notorious of all the settlements in England's new American colonies. Its history resembles those of the boom towns that later sprang up almost overnight in the West of the United States.

Sermons were preached in London when the first ships brought news of the destruction of Port Royal, Jamaica, by earthquake, in 1692. The "pirate" capital of the West Indies, Port Royal had also been called the wickedest city in the world and "the dunghill of the universe, the refuse of whole creation, . . . the receptacle of vagabonds, the sanctuary of bankrupts, and a close-stool for the purges of our prisons. As sickly as a hospital, as dangerous as the plague, as hot as Hell, and as wicked as the devil. Subject to tornadoes, hurricanes and earthquakes, as if the island and the people were troubled with the dry belly-ache."

In that time people talked much about religion and seldom acted like Christians. Port Royal's collapse into the sea was thought to be the act of God in His wrath. So angered was He considered to be by the town's iniquity that He caused the earth to tremble and destroy the town. The idea created a religious panic. For a time, English churches were packed with people who hoped to make peace with God before He rose in vengeance against them too. The fact that the same earthquake brought destruction to Jamaican towns far distant from Port Royal was not mentioned. The rest of the island did not have Port Royal's fame and so was not the subject of sermons. Port Royal was England's richest outpost, and it had a fearsome reputation.

And yet, less than forty years before the town was destroyed, it was nothing but an uninhabited sandbar.

At first a military outpost surrounded by enemies (in this case Spaniards rather than Indians), Port Royal flourished suddenly when a great source of wealth was discovered—wealth in gold and silver and other precious materials. But this wealth was not taken from the soil of Jamaica, for which Port Royal was the principal harbor. It was taken from the Spaniards, whose empire the English had invaded (just as the Spaniards had invaded the same territory earlier to plunder the Indian empires).

When the English first took Jamaica from the Spanish, the site of Port Royal was nothing but a hot, barren sandbar which had the advantage of overlooking the large harbor that served the old Spanish capital of Sant' Jago de la Vega. The English renamed this capital Spanish Town and used it for a while as their headquarters. Forts were erected on the sandbar, then named Cagua. It soon became obvious that Cagua, with its deep water close to the beach, was an excellent place to bring in ships to protect them from enemies and tropical storms, and a place to beach ships so that their bottoms could be scraped clean of barnacles. A town grew up on Cagua, and the site was renamed Port Royal.

This new town soon attracted buccaneers, whom the Spanish

called pirates. Surrounded as it was by Spanish colonies, the weak English outpost welcomed these men as a defense against attack.

Buccaneers were not the type of men to explain where they came from. From England, France, Holland and various colonies they had made their way, starting in the early 1600s, to the north coast of Santo Domingo, claimed by Spain but rarely occupied by it. Most of the buccaneers were no doubt fugitives, escaped debtors, convicts or indentured servants, or deserters from the harsh military life of the time. None of them was from Spain. Hatred of that nation, learned during Europe's religious wars between Protestants and Catholics, was one of the things that united these rugged individualists.

At first the buccaneers did not engage in piracy. They lived by hunting the wild cattle and pigs introduced to Santo Domingo from Spain. They cured their meat by a smoking process that the Indians called *boucan*, the source of their name. Their own name for themselves was "the Brethren of the Coast." They elected their leaders democratically. In time their head man was called "Admiral." Everything was owned in common, including their women.

When the Spaniards in the town of Santo Domingo had learned of these squatters on the north coast of the island, they sent soldiers to drive them out. The north coast is rugged and mountainous, and the buccaneers were tough. Unable to defeat them in battle, the Spanish troops slaughtered the wild livestock which was the buccaneers' main source of food. This policy succeeded in driving the buccaneers out. They then sailed to the unoccupied island of Tortuga, off the north shore of Santo Domingo. From there the Brethren began to take to the sea in earnest. They developed a method of attacking ships, preferably Spanish ones, that proved enormously successful. Attaching one sail to a canoe gave them a swift, maneuverable craft that could often sail faster than its lumbering victim. The buccaneers would maneuver themselves under the stern of a ship to avoid its guns—which could fire broadside only—throw grappling irons aboard, climb up, surprise the crew and make the ship captive. Often the attacks were made at night.

Much has been made of the cruelty of the buccaneers, but these were cruel times. In England, for instance, there were two hundred crimes for which the punishment was death. Mutilation of criminals was common. Torture was a regular instrument of the law. Executions of courtiers frequently occurred during the reign of Elizabeth I, and King Charles I was beheaded in 1649. All the nations colonizing the Americas were engaged in slave trading, with unspeakable horrors in the slave ships, but no one in these Christian nations raised a protest. If the buccaneers killed in pursuit of their prizes, they were no more brutal than the English courts or the Spanish Inquisition, which committed legal murder. Terrorists or not, the buccaneers prospered and acquired a fleet of first-class ships.

The words "buccaneer" and "pirate" are almost interchangeable, and both are confused with a third term, "privateer." Strictly speaking, buccaneers were simply hunters among the island frontiers who had taken to sea and preyed almost entirely on Spaniards. Pirates were considered something worse than buccaneers because they respected no nationality and would attack any ship they felt they could overcome. Whenever any of these men, pirates or buccaneers, received commissions from the English or the French, they were called privateers and they acted completely within the law. To add to the language confusion, ships of the British and French Royal navies were also commissioned as privateers, and they raided for plunder just as buccaneers did. The single difference between privateers and other plunderers was that privateers were legal.

The buccaneer or privateer most remembered today was Sir Henry Morgan, a Welshman who terrorized the Spaniards for many years. There are no records of his early life, and he never mentioned it. He just suddenly appears in recorded history in 1662, when he received a privateer's commission at Port Royal.

He must have had previous experience with buccaneers at Tortuga, for he brought many men and ships from there to Port Royal, where they received commissions to ply their trade lawfully. Morgan considered himself a loyal Englishman, and most of his recruits were English, too.

Port Royal attracted these buccaneers for many reasons. It was English, while Tortuga was a melting pot of people from almost all Europe, and the English of the time considered all foreigners rather suspect. Port Royal was also a town, while Tortuga was nothing but a wild outpost. In Port Royal the men could sell whatever precious metals, jewels, pearls, rich fabrics or other cargoes they had captured to an ever-growing band of willing merchants. The buccaneers (or privateers) sold their goods for pieces of eight at ridiculously low prices, and the merchants transshipped their purchases to London to be sold at great profit. Some of the privateers, such as Morgan, kept a good deal of their money and invested it in plantations. But most of them spent their sudden wealth as sailors always have, in drink, women, gambling—in general, wild abandon. Life at sea was hard and dangerous; those who got back to the port alive wanted to savor existence to the full. Most of them had grown up poor, and instant riches made them lose their heads. It was the behavior of these men ashore, and the many taverns and women who so willingly accepted their money, that gave Port Royal its reputation for wickedness.

The merchants who profited from this disreputable trade tried, as they grew wealthy, to act more and more like members of the respectable English middle class. They imported fine furniture, silver, china and glassware from England and the Continent. They imported English bricks to build English-style houses in the tropics. They wore heavy English clothes. They built a church. They began to raise families. Attempts were made by this element to establish law and order among a population that was mostly lawless and rootless. (There are many parallels in these developments with those of towns in the American West.)

These merchants also engaged in the importing and selling of

Negro slaves from West Africa. This trade was slow in getting started, since at first the Dutch held almost a complete monopoly of the trade, protected by their Navy, which patrolled the African coast and drove foreigners out. The English had to engage in three brief wars with the Dutch before this monopoly could be broken, and then Port Royal became one of the largest slave markets of the West Indies. It was believed that no Englishman could survive the hot, heavy work in the sugar-care fields and so sugar cultivation could never prosper without slaves from Africa. In Europe a large market for sugar existed. Once enough slaves existed to produce large amounts of sugar, Jamaica seemed to have a much sounder basis for prosperity than when it survived on the fruits of the privateering trade.

The raucous community named Port Royal no longer exists, but what went on there, and from there, had effects that are still very much with us today. The daring raids of the privateers on Spanish territory showed that the feared Spanish Empire was really very weak. The defeats Spain suffered were the first she had ever had in the Americas, and the nation never won another victory in North or South America. The power of Spain went on shrinking and declining until all the Spanish lands in the Americas were free from European control. The United States then was able to acquire an enormous territory once claimed by Spain, the Louisiana Territory, and later the land known as Florida. Of course, Morgan and his men did not destroy the Spanish Empire single-handedly, but their deeds were like a stone dropped into a pool which causes ripples to spread widely from the point of impact. In the local history of the Caribbean, solidification of the English possession of Jamaica had very long-term effects, as anyone can tell who visits that beautiful island today.

Few towns of significance can have had such a short life span as Port Royal. None can have been so colorful. The pity is that, although much is known about Port Royal, all the written records in the town itself and most other physical evidence were destroyed in the final disaster. Some documents about Port Royal have been found in Spanish Town, with which it shared the title of capital. Other records can be found in official files in London, and some letters remain in the archives of various English families. Some material can be found in Barbados, New England, New York and Madrid. So much is gone, however, that would be fascinating to know about. There have been enough romances written about pirates and such. This book is written about Port Royal and its era, with very few adjectives supplied by the author. The times, the same as those when the North American colonies were being founded, have color enough of their own.

The Conquest of Jamaica

Christopher Columbus, whose voyages ultimately caused more turmoil, more controversies and wars between nations than any other trips ever taken, found the north shore of Jamaica in 1494, during his second cruise through the West Indies. He took the island in the name of King Ferdinand and Queen Isabella of Spain, but he did not occupy it. Columbus' description of the island as it was then was recorded by the Spanish historian Andrés Bernaldez:

> It is the fairest island eyes have ever beheld; mountainous and the land seems to touch the sky; very large, bigger than Sicily, has a circumference of 800 leagues, and all full of valleys and fields and plains; it is very strong and extraordinarily populous; even on the edge of the sea as well as inland it is full of very big villages very near together, about four leagues apart.

16

In 1503 Columbus returned to the north shore of Jamaica, and he was stranded there for twelve months after he lost his ship. But permanent Spanish settlement did not begin until 1509, when a party of colonists from Santo Domingo arrived, led by Juan de Esquevil.

The people already living on the island were a peaceful race of Indians known as the Arawaks. They had probably migrated to Jamaica from the Guiana area of South America, where Arawak Indians still exist today. They were short people, copper colored, with somewhat flat noses and straight black hair, who were inclined to be plump. They slept in hammocks. Arawaks did not know about bows and arrows. Their only weapons were spears, often tipped with sharks' teeth. Estimates of the Arawak population of Jamaica around 1509 range between 60,000 and 100,000 people. The men were skilled fishermen and also caught the huge sea turtles that were then plentiful. Women did the farming. The rich soil and the semitropical climate produced sufficient food with very little effort. The major crops were corn, cassava and sweet potatoes.

The Spanish settlers who arrived were, of course, eager for gold and silver. When they discovered that the Arawaks could not produce these metals for them they were disappointed. Esquevil did bring in sugar cane, however, and he enslaved the Indians to grow the cane. The experiment with the Arawaks was not a success. During the 146 years of Spanish rule on Jamaica, every single Arawak died, either from one of the diseases the white men brought, from Spanish brutality or from despair at the idea of being a slave. By the time the English arrived in 1655 the Arawaks had vanished. Meanwhile, the Spanish had begun to make up for the loss of Indian labor by importing Negro slaves from Africa.

Jamaica, naturally, did not exist in a vacuum. It was just one of many lands in the Americas that became pawns in the deadly games of European politics. Unlike Mexico and Peru, Jamaica had no great stores of mineral wealth to be plundered, so Spain

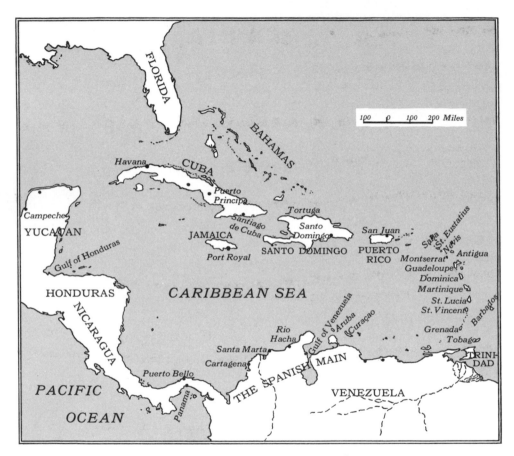

The Caribbean in the mid-seventeenth century

never paid it much attention. But its location was strategically important. It lay across the major trade routes of the Caribbean, where treasure ships from Mexico and Panama had to sail, and it was within easy striking distance of most major Spanish outposts. Spain held it, however loosely, mostly to deny any other nation access to it. Although Spain was the military terror of Europe during the sixteenth century, it actually concealed great internal weakness and was unable to fortify strongly the lands it claimed across the Atlantic.

Spain believed it had the right to possess all the western world. This belief started with Columbus, who claimed his discoveries for Spain, and was reinforced by an edict of Pope Alexander VI, one of the Borgias and a Spaniard by birth. This edict stated that a north-to-south "line" would divide the western world, and that everything west of the line would belong to Spain. Everything east of the line, which included most of Brazil, was given to Portugal. Spain soon announced that no other nation could settle, trade or even travel in her lands.

Neither France nor Holland nor England ever accepted the Pope's line. They were, though, late starters in the game of American conquest. (This was true as well in India, the rest of Asia and the Pacific Ocean.) They intended to catch up, however, and this led to bloodshed in the Americas from the time of the piracy of the Englishman Sir Francis Drake, which began in 1572, to the time when a former British colony, the United States, destroyed the last vestiges of the Spanish Empire in the West Indies and the Pacific in 1898.

One of the early events in this long struggle to divide up the western world was Spain's attempt in 1588 to crush England once and for all. King Philip II of Spain outfitted a great Armada of 130 ships and about thirty thousand men to destroy the English fleet and invade England. The Spanish suffered a terrible defeat, and a hatred of Spain was created among Englishmen. If the Spanish had successfully invaded England, Philip II would have restored Catholicism to England, which had recently broken away from the Church of Rome and established the Church of England. The knowledge of Philip's intent to bring back Catholicism added fuel to the flame in Protestant English hearts. The age of religious wars was not over.

Twenty years after the defeat of the Armada, France, Holland and England all had colonies in the New World. There were numerous battles between these various settlements, all the way from Canada to Guiana in South America. Various settlements changed hands a number of times. As the story of Port Royal begins, however—in 1654—France had settlers in Canada, Guadeloupe, Martinique, one half of St. Kitts and what is now Haiti. The Dutch held Curaçao, Saba, St. Eustatius, and the Hudson River Valley in what is now the state of New York. The British controlled New England, Virginia, Barbados, the other half of St. Kitts, Antigua, Montserrat and Nevis. The fighting Carib Indians held on to St. Lucia, Dominica and St. Vincent, and none of these islands seemed desirable enough yet to the European powers to move the Indians out. Spain's interest in the Caribbean lay in the larger islands—Trinidad, Puerto Rico, Santo Domingo, Cuba and Jamaica—and in the mainland of America from Mexico south. Buccaneers controlled the island of Tortuga, off the north coast of Santo Domingo.

It was Oliver Cromwell who, in 1654, decided to open hostilities with Spain and accidentally changed the fate of Jamaica.

Cromwell was the military dictator of England, called the "Lord Protector." He had assumed that title only the year before. As a Puritan Member of Parliament he had opposed Charles I of the house of Stuart, who believed in the theory that the king had a divine right to rule. At the same time Parliament, made up largely of middle-class Puritans and Presbyterians, was trying to increase its power. It declared that only Parliament could raise taxes, that there could be no imprisonment without cause, no quartering of soldiers in citizens' houses and no martial law in time of peace. The angry King had dissolved Parliament and ruled without it for eleven years. He finally had to recall it, however, because he discovered that he could not in fact raise money without a legislature.

The new Parliament was even more eager than the old one to curb the King's power and, to enforce its demands, it began to raise an army. The Stuart King quickly raised a military force himself, and a civil war soon broke out between the Roundheads (the Puritan Army) and the Cavaliers (the supporters of the King). Cromwell showed himself to be a very skilled and lucky commander and defeated the Cavalier forces in the battles of Edgehill, Marston Moor and Naseby.

The deposed King Charles was executed in 1649. A troubled England had relative peace for a while. Cromwell, however, led the Puritan Army into Scotland to subdue rebellion there, led invaded Ireland in a very bloody expedition that has made his name hated in that country ever since. Then, as commander in chief of the Puritan Army, Cromwell began to have his own troubles with Parliament, whose members were generally not Puritans, and he dissolved it in 1653. He announced a Protectorate in its place and the Army proclaimed him Lord Protector. The Army collected the taxes, and the Lord Protector began a Puritanical rule that soon made him very unpopular. He punished sinners as well as criminals. He abolished Christmas as a celebration. It was not a rule destined to last very long, but it did have its advocates, among them the poet John Milton, who published a pamphlet in praise of the execution of King Charles immediately after the deed. As a reward for his support and because of his skill as a writer, Milton was named the government's "Latin secretary." In this capacity he wrote broadsides defending the Protectorate, in Latin, and corresponded with foreign governments in the same language.

Milton wrote the documents concerning a brief war Cromwell waged with Holland and then, in 1654, although already totally blind, Milton dictated a manifesto, at Cromwell's order, that accidentally changed the fate of Jamaica. The document did not actually declare war. But it did announce that, because of the state and condition of the English plantations and colonies in the western part of the world called America, an expeditionary force would be sent to secure "the interest we already have in those countries, which now lie open and exposed to the will and power of the King of Spain (who claims the same by colour of a donation of the Pope) at any time when he shall have the leisure to look that way, and also for getting ground and gaining upon the dominions and territories of the said King there; Whereunto we also hold ourself obliged in justice to the people of these nations for the cruelties, wrongs and injuries done and exercised upon them by the Spaniards in those parts."

The manifesto went on to complain of the "miserable thraldom and bondage both spiritual and physical . . . of the Popish and cruel Inquisition." (This was the Spanish religious court that burned heretics.) Cromwell declared his intent to deliver the colonies held by Spain in the Americas, and to bring in "the light of the Gospel and power of true religion and Godliness in those parts." He stated that this would be the most glorious result of any acquisition the expedition might make. A military commander of great skill, Cromwell had established his own brand of Christianity in the British Isles by virtue of winning battles, and he obviously believed God would like to see the Americas established as Puritan outposts by the same means. God would also approve of the English taking additional territory at the expense of Spain.

Hit-and-run attacks on Spanish ships and Spanish towns in the Americas were already no novelty in 1654. The buccaneers kept no records of the number of ships they were capturing, but their successes must have been considerable, because they were able to show a quite sizeable fleet a few years later when they joined forces with the English in Jamaica.

Privateering against the Spanish had often had the sanction of governments, and expeditions were often financed by prominent men. In 1628, the Dutch sent Admiral Piet Hein as a privateer with a fleet to harass the Spaniards in the Caribbean. Admiral Hein stationed his ships off the harbor of Matanzas in northern Cuba and managed one of the great coups of the century. He captured one whole Spanish treasure fleet—nine galleons loaded with tropical produce and eight ships whose load of silver weighed some 200,000 pounds. The value of this capture was more than $10 million.

Before its conquest by the English, Jamaica had twice been attacked by invaders. In 1596 a swashbuckler named Sir Anthony Shirley stormed the capital, Sant' Jago de la Vega. He plundered the town and then burned it. In 1643 another Englishman, Captain William Jackson, arrived in the harbor with three ships. Sant' Jago was captured from the Spanish a second time and ransomed. Among Jackson's booty were seven thousand pieces of eight, two hundred cattle and thousands of loaves of cassava bread—a rather tasteless food, but one that kept well aboard ships.

When Cromwell decided to obtain "an establishment in the West Indies which is possessed by the Spaniards," he settled on Santo Domingo, and he chose men to lead the invasion whose fighting qualities he thought he knew.

General Robert Venables had been with the Puritan Army ever since the beginning of the Civil Wars, and, during the five years before the invasion to conquer Santo Domingo, he had served Cromwell in Ireland.

The other leader, Admiral Sir William Penn, had spent his entire career as a sailor. His first known command of a Navy ship came when he was only twenty-three. He was loyal to Cromwell during the fighting in Ireland and had commanded the fleet during a brief war Cromwell had waged against the Dutch. Then, it seems, Penn had a change of heart. Royalist sympathies overwhelmed him, and just before the invasion of the West Indies he offered to deliver the English fleet to any port on the Continent named by Charles II, exiled son of the dead Charles I. The young Stuart heir was continually plotting to regain the throne, but he did not consider the time ripe, so he declined Penn's offer. (When the monarchy was restored, in 1660, Penn was one of the officers who went to Holland to escort Charles II back to England. As a reward, many political turns later, Penn's son, William, was given the tract of land in America which he named Pennsylvania.)

The project to take Santo Domingo started out with some difficulties. The command was divided and, as far as the orders could be understood, Admiral Penn and General Venables had equal authority. This naturally increased the rivalry common between all armies and navies.

Venables asked for soldiers that he had commanded in Ireland, but he knew hardly any of the men he was actually given. Fewer than a thousand of them were veterans. One of the men in the company described the others as "Hectors [bullies] and knights of the blade, with common cheats, thieves, cutpurses and such lewd persons who had long time lived by the slight of hand and dexterity of wit, and were now making a fair progress unto Newgate [London's prison], from whence they were to proceed towards Tiborn [Tyburn, the hanging ground]." Venables himself described his army as "unruly raw soldiers, the major part ignorant, lazy, dull—officers that have a large portion of pride, but not of wit, valour or activity."

This unpromising expeditionary force arrived off Barbados in January, 1655. The little island of Barbados was already a well-established English colony with more than thirty thousand whites and about six thousand Negroes. It exported millions of dollars' worth of sugar every year. The planter society was a brutal and drunken one. A visitor, describing their principal beverage, said, "The chief fuddling they make in the island is Rumbullion, alias Kill-Devil, and this is made of sugar canes distilled, a hot, hellish and terrible liquor."

The Barbadians had a political assembly, mostly Royalist in feeling, and very contentious. They objected to orders from

Parliament in London and said that to be ruled by "a Parliament in which we have no representatives . . . would be a slavery exceeding all that the English nation hath yet suffered." Barbados was the first colony to raise the cry "No taxation without representation." In practice, the Barbadians seldom paid the taxes that the Commonwealth considered its due.

Penn and Venables stayed at Barbados for ten weeks, during which time their troops practically ate the island out of food. The leaders felt they needed a larger force, so, with the aid of Governor Thomas Modyford, they raised thousands more troops from among the indentured servants. These men, who had signed away their lives in return for passage from England to America, earned their freedom by enlisting. Modyford and other large landowners were glad to be rid of them, since Barbados had become overpopulated. In addition, for workers, they preferred slaves from Africa.

From Barbados the British force sailed to Santo Domingo. Aboard the thirty-eight ships were about eight thousand men, one family—the Barretts*—and General Venables' young second wife. Venables was planning to settle down and become a rich landowner immediately after the conquest.

The attack on Santo Domingo was a disaster. The Spanish defenders knew the English were coming and were well prepared to meet them. The army landed too far from the town of Santo Domingo, thirty miles away. Penn gave Venables no gunfire support from his ships. The English army lacked ammunition and was poorly supplied with food and water. It was badly defeated by a much smaller Spanish force and was saved from complete destruction only by a professional regiment of marines, part of Penn's forces.

Neither Penn nor Venables seemed to dare return to England

---

*The head of this family, Hersey Barrett, was a direct ancestor of the poet Elizabeth Barrett, who married Robert Browning. Hersey Barrett's family was eventually to prosper, not in Santo Domingo but in Jamaica. Browning's family also derived its wealth from Jamaica.

and face Cromwell's wrath. Judging that it was also necessary to raise the troops' morale by "some success in a small exploit," they "resolved to attempt some other plantation, and at last Jamaica was pitched on to be the place."

On May 10, 1655, the convoy sailed past the site soon to become Port Royal and into what is now known as Kingston Harbour. They had been sighted when some distance away by two fishermen who paddled their swift canoes to shore in time to raise an alarm. The English ships anchored in the harbor out of range of gunfire. This time, fearing a repetition of Santo Domingo, which disaster was led primarily by General Venables, Admiral Penn took charge. He ordered one of his smallest ships—it carried only twelve guns and sixty men—to lead the assault and travel up the Caguaya River as far as it could go.

The Spanish capital in Jamaica, Sant' Jago de la Vega, was six miles from the harbor. A breastwork, hardly a fort, at the little town of Caguaya on the river was the capital's main protection against attack from the sea. The small ship, the *Martin*, went up the river and anchored within range of the breastwork. Shots were exchanged by the ship and the shore, but little damage was done by either side.

Penn and Venables were soon rowed to the *Martin* in a small boat. Quickly the ship was surrounded by all the other English vessels that could get into the shallow river. Their decks were crowded with soldiers ready to land.

Later it was learned that most of the residents of Caguaya were away that day, working on their sugar plantations, cacao groves or cattle ranches. Only the governor, with five iron cannons and 180 men, was on the beach to oppose the invasion. When the British began to come ashore the Spanish fled, leaving behind three guns and a few wounded men.

Venables did not lead his men into what might have been a battle, but stayed aboard the *Martin*, pacing the deck, wrapped up in a cloak. Venables was very ill at this time from some unnamed malady. He may also have had little faith in his soldiers and have been worried about the safety of his wife. In the afternoon, however, he did go ashore, but he refused, in spite of the advice of his officers, to advance to Sant' Jago that day. The troops spent the night in Caguaya and marched on the small capital the next morning. They found no opposition. Venables established himself in the town hall, and his officers took other buildings in the town.

Later in the day two Spanish officers appeared at the town hall under a flag of truce. One was named Ysassi and the other Duarte de Acosta. They accepted a document outlining the terms of peace, but begged for time to consider it before signing. They considered it for several days while their fellow Spaniards hastily removed most of their valuables, freed their slaves and fled through the almost impenetrable mountain country to the north shore.* The total population of Spaniards and slaves in Sant' Jago was no more than 1,500, including about 200 soldiers. After signing the treaty at last, Ysassi and Acosta also hurried north, where they established a base from which Ysassi soon began a campaign of guerrilla warfare.

Penn and Venables had won a notable victory of sorts—eight thousand Englishmen and thirty-eight ships against 200 Spanish soldiers. But, though they had conquered a Spanish island, it was not the one Cromwell desired, and both men still feared his reaction.

Jamaica was conquered on May 11, and Penn waited only until June 25 before sailing home. Probably he departed in his ship, the *Swiftsure*, without consulting Venables. Delayed by ill health (he almost died in Jamaica), Venables did not embark for London

---

*Not all of the Spanish escaped so readily, however. The English had heard of a "rich fat woman, the richest of the country," Doña Joana de Fuentes, whom they succeeded in capturing, along with her nephew and some slaves. The nephew was sent to get all Doña de Fuentes' money and jewels as ransom, and the spoil was divided among a captain, a lieutenant and an ensign.

until July 4, aboard the *Marston Moor*. He was anxious to see Cromwell before Penn had completely prejudiced the Lord Protector about the causes of the disaster at Santo Domingo.

Penn reached England on August 31 and was almost immediately imprisoned in the Tower of London. The charge against him was that he had come home without leave. Venables arrived on September 9 and, after a hearing, was also committed to the Tower on the same charge.

After a brief stay in the Tower, Penn was released. He retired to Ireland, where he plotted with the Royalists for the restoration of Charles II. Venables was released on October 30, after resigning his commission as general. Soon he too enlisted in the Royalist cause.

Early Struggles

While British forces were attacking Spanish possessions in the West Indies, Cromwell's ambassador in Madrid was trying to reach a treaty of amity with Spain, since Cromwell believed France to be England's true enemy. The ambassador asked that his country's ships be allowed to trade in Spanish ports and that British sailors be allowed to practice their Puritan religion in Spanish territory.

Even if the Spanish monarchy had not been extremely hostile to Cromwell's regicide republic, they still would have considered these terms outrageous. Considering the rigid Spanish attitude toward any foreigners in her colonies, the ambassador's task was probably hopeless. Failure was guaranteed, however, when the court heard about the British attacks on Santo Domingo and Jamaica. Instead of a treaty, the ambassador received a declaration of war on October 3.

Cromwell could not have been expecting his ambassador to negotiate a satisfactory treaty with Spain, because on October 10, before Cromwell had even heard that Spain had declared war, he issued a proclamation that could only infuriate the Spanish more. Although Cromwell had imprisoned and then dismissed Penn and Venables, he was delighted that they had taken Jamaica. His proclamation on October 10 urged that all interested English subjects transplant themselves to Jamaica. He offered free land, waived taxes for a number of years and guaranteed the colonists all the rights of Englishmen. He called Jamaica "a land of plenty." He sent a special proclamation to New England urging colonists in that "desert and barren wilderness" to remove themselves to the Garden of Eden which British forces had just won. (Massachusetts was not popular in England. What produce it exported competed with that grown at home. Even worse, the colonists were showing symptoms of the independent spirit that finally caused so much trouble for George III.)

Soon after this proclamation was issued, Cromwell received the news of Spain's declaration of war. On October 23, he replied with a formal announcement of hostilities.

In fact the formal proclamations of the two countries' governments made little difference in the West Indies. Spanish and British nationals fought constantly anyway, paying little attention to the policies laid down in Europe.

Cromwell's glowing description of Jamaica was more propaganda than fact. The island was surrounded by hostile Spanish islands from which an invasion might be launched at any time. The remaining Spanish colonists and the freed Negro slaves in Jamaica were engaged in bloody guerrilla attacks on the British. Worse, the infant British colony was in danger of collapsing from disease, lack of food and terrible military discipline.

Before Admiral Penn had left Jamaica in June, while General Venables was hovering between life and death, he had drawn up a commission which named Major General Richard Fortescue as the new commander in chief. Then Penn appointed William Goodson to be his successor as admiral and commander in chief of the fleet.

Fortescue was a good officer, popular with the soldiers and very pious. The Lord Protector wrote him, "I do commend, in the midst of others' miscarriages, your constancy and faithfulness to your trust in every situation where you are and you taking care of 'a company of poor sheep left by their shepherd.'"

Commendations from Cromwell were fine, but Fortescue had troubles. His pay was in arrears and his wife in England needed money. His troops, having been abandoned by the original leaders of the expedition, were in a very bad state of morale. They would not do any planting, fearing that if they did so they would never be released from duty on the island. Also they feared attack from Spanish guerrillas and freed slaves, and in fact a number of men were killed by these enemies.

With no food being produced in Jamaica, and with the half rations with which the troops had arrived fast disappearing, provisions soon became very scarce. Tropical diseases, probably malaria and yellow fever, were killing off many of the troops. The unaccustomed heat was particularly debilitating to the men, whose heavy clothes were suitable for England but not for the Caribbean in the summer.

Fortescue wrote of Jamaica to a friend in London. He praised the island as a place of opportunity for godly men, then added:

> Many there are that came out with us vaunting, as if they would have carried the Indies, big with expectation of gold and silver ready tied up in bags. Not finding that, but meeting with some difficulties and hardships, wherewith God uses to try and exercise his people, they fret, fume and grow impatient. . . . Several of such, according to their desires and discontents, we have dismissed and may return with shame enough. We expect in their own defence they will disparage the place and service, but I hope wise and sober men will not give much credit to them.

Admiral Goodson, meanwhile, was carrying on the work of harrying the Spanish. On July 31 he sailed with a fleet of nine ships and raided the town of Santa Marta on the coast of what is now Colombia. Santa Marta had only two little forts and about two hundred houses. Goodson's men sacked the town and shared the booty, as was the custom. It was more profitable for men to go to sea than to try to make a life farming land in Jamaica.

Even before news of the conquest of Jamaica had reached England, Cromwell realized that Penn and Venables would need reinforcements. To lead them Cromwell chose General Robert Sedgwick. Sedgwick had emigrated to Massachusetts in 1635, at the age of twenty-four. He settled in Charlestown and became a merchant. Later he moved to Boston, became captain of an artillery company and, in 1652, major general of the colony. He built ships, warehouses and docks and lived as a busy citizen.

Then, on a visit to England, Sedgwick was commissioned by Cromwell to take New Netherlands from the Dutch. But peace with Holland was declared before Sedgwick could carry out his orders. He recruited troops in Massachusetts anyway and, from there, proceeded north and took Acadia, now Nova Scotia, from the French. When he returned to England Cromwell named him commissioner of civil affairs in Jamaica.

Sedgwick sailed on July 11, 1655, with a squadron of ships and a regiment of eight hundred men, to join Penn and Venables. He arrived at Barbados on August 27 without having lost a single man. This was considered remarkable at that time when deaths were expected on every voyage.

In Barbados, Sedgwick learned of Penn's and Venables' failure at Santo Domingo and their success at Jamaica. He took food aboard, then sailed by Santo Domingo. Later he reported that he could have captured Santo Domingo with far fewer men than Penn and Venables had under their command.

Communications were so slow in that age that it was not until Sedgwick arrived in Jamaica on October 1 that he learned that

Penn and Venables were gone, although they had left four months previously. Sedgwick, the new civilian commissioner, discovered that the new military commissioners, General Fortescue and Admiral Goodson, had become rivals over the same question that had troubled Penn and Venables: who had the greater authority?

At first Sedgwick favored Goodson, but then all three men met aboard the frigate *Torrington* and, after a heated discussion that lasted for several days, reached a compromise in which all of them agreed to work for the good of the infant colony. Then, a few days later, Fortescue died of one of the fevers for which the colonists had no immunity or remedies. He had survived just six months in the tropics.

Sedgwick soon reported to London that many officers had deserted their posts, that others were dead and that still others were so sick that they were incapable of command. He said that a great number of soldiers had died and some of their carcasses lay on the roads unburied, that still living soldiers walked around like ghosts, while others lay on the ground, groaning and crying out.

At the same time Admiral Goodson wrote to London: "The Army is in a deplorable condition by the death of General Fortescue." (The sailors, for the most part, remained in good health, probably because, living aboard ship, they were less exposed to the fevers so prevalent in Jamaica.) Goodson and Sedgwick then put Colonel Edward D'Oyley in charge of those soldiers who still remained alive.

In spite of all these troubles, Sedgwick found time and courage to write to Cromwell: "This kind of marooning cruising West Indies trade of plundering and burning of towns, though it has long been practiced in these parts, . . . is not honorable for a princely navy, neither was it, I think, the work designed, though perhaps it may be tolerated at present." This unsolicited opinion was brave, since Sedgwick must have known that it was the Lord Protector's fond policy to harass the Spaniards. What Sedgwick said when Admiral Goodson and his fleet sailed out of Jamaica in

April, 1656, to sack the town of Río Hacha on the north coast of South America is not known, for Sedgwick died the following month. Many of the replacements he had brought with him had already perished.

In December of that year General Brayne arrived with 1,000 troops, to replace Sedgwick. The next month Admiral Goodson, on orders from home, sailed back to England with his fleet. Brayne survived until September, 1657, only ten months. Colonel D'Oyley, the man chosen by Sedgwick and Goodson to take over Fortescue's command of the army, found himself alone and in charge, without any direct orders from home.

The colony was certainly in desperate condition by 1657, yet somehow it managed to survive. Colonists arrived from England, from Barbados and from the island of Nevis, although Jamaica had a well-earned reputation for bad health. No settlers arrived from Massachusetts, in spite of Cromwell's urging.

Jamaica had lacked a navy since Goodson's departure, and was wide open to attack. D'Oyley gave commissions to the buccaneers who were living on Tortuga, so that they might become legal privateers and give his small outpost some protection against the Spanish. He must therefore be given the credit, or the ill fame, for establishing Jamaica's first source of prosperity.

D'Oyley had a continuing problem with the Spanish, who still claimed Jamaica and remained on Jamaica's north coast. Ysassi, who had signed the treaty with Penn and Venables at Sant' Jago in 1655, had been named governor of the island by Spain. With his few troops he frequently conducted guerrilla raids on outlying English plantations. Help in these forays often came from the Negro slaves who had been liberated at the time of the British conquest. Known as Maroons, these former slaves were fiercely independent, but thought Spain the lesser of two evils. They lived in an inaccessible area known as the Cockpit country, and the British conquerors found it almost impossible to dislodge them.

In 1657, approaching the north coast from the sea, D'Oyley and his troops fought Ysassi and his men at Ocho Ríos. In 1658, D'Oyley fought Ysassi again at Río Nuevo. In theory the English were victorious, but Ysassi's power was not destroyed.

Then, in 1660, D'Oyley learned from a friendly Negro that Ysassi still remained in the north, pretending that he was the legal ruler of the island. The English had not yet occupied the north at all, so Ysassi could easily hide there. D'Oyley sent a force of eighty men under Colonel Tyson against him. This time the English advanced overland and, after a very difficult march across the mountains, found Ysassi with more than one hundred men encamped in a swamp.

Ysassi was not well at the time, and the Spanish were led by his second in command, Raspuru. The English, though outnumbered, advanced boldly. Raspuru received a mortal wound from a lance almost immediately. Ysassi ran away so quickly that he was not captured. Fifty Spanish were killed, however, and others were captured. Not a single English soldier died. Those few Spaniards who escaped with Ysassi embarked in dugout canoes and sailed to Cuba. The place from which they departed is now known as Runaway Bay.

Two years before this encounter, Ysassi had written to the Viceroy of the Spanish colonies in America, the Duke of Albuquerque: "So long as ships of force do not come that can give trouble to the enemy on sea, the island cannot be restored, because although I might press him by land, as master of the sea he will throw troops on me as he does, wherever it may suit him, hindering me from getting the reliefs that can come to me by sea for the sustenance of my infantry."

The Spanish were acutely aware of the value of sea power, but did not have ships enough to attempt the recovery of Jamaica. D'Oyley did not know this, and he expected that the Spanish would eventually attack the island from the sea. He looked for every possible means of protecting his capital at Spanish Town, as Sant' Jago was beginning to be known. To approach the town from the sea, ships had to go through a rather narrow strait and past an island known as Cagua. D'Oyley began to fortify this island, and a little community that became the town of Port Royal began to develop.

III

Privateers and Planters

The fortifications on Cagua which were begun by D'Oyley finally made Jamaica's largest harbor almost impregnable. No ship ever managed to make its way in by force. The location of the island had another asset, besides commanding the entrance to the harbor. The water on the landward side of the island was very deep and the largest ships of the time could come right up to the beach. There, when wharves were built, the ships could easily discharge their cargoes. Ships could also sail up to the beach for careening. (To careen a ship was to cause it to go aground deliberately, then tip it over on its side so that the bottom could be scrubbed clean of barnacles.) A further advantage of the location was that, once inside the harbor it protected, ships were safe from violent storms and hurricanes.

In spite of these virtues, however, the place where Port Royal began to grow was a very unwise choice for a large town. In spite of being on the sea, it was very hot. Local rumor has it that this area gets more sunshine than any other place in the West Indies. The local water was very brackish, and often those who drank it got sick. There was no wood available except for the mangrove trees that grew in the island's swamps. No food could be grown on Cagua itself, and at first everything had to be brought there from Jamaica. Some years later, however, the land just to the east of Port Royal rose a few feet and a road to Jamaica could be built.

Some of the island of Cagua is made of limestone, but most of it is sand. Apparently no Englishman thought about it or perhaps no one knew it, but the area is subject to earthquakes. The Spanish may have realized this, because they raised no buildings more than one story high. On the sandy base of Cagua, however, the English built three-story houses made of brick imported from England. As the town of Port Royal began to grow, land was filled in on the harbor side of the island. The engineering methods of the time were rather primitive, and the man-made land was hardly a secure foundation for buildings.

Both merchant ships and the English Navy used Port Royal, and very soon buccaneers were to use it, too. Captain Mings of the Navy sailed from Port Royal to raid the Spanish Main in 1659. This swashbuckling man had begun life at sea as a cabin boy and, in spite of having none of the aristocratic connections that were usually necessary for advancement as an officer, had risen to high rank very rapidly. Mings attacked the towns of Cumaná and Santa Ana de Coro on the mainland of what is now Venezuela and brought back twelve thousand pieces of eight. Although Colonel D'Oyley had authorized privateers to attack Spanish ships, he apparently felt that towns were not legal game. He suspended Captain Mings and sent him back to England in the *Marston Moor*, under arrest.

Oliver Cromwell died in 1659, and his son Richard succeeded

him. But Richard Cromwell's rule was short and unsuccessful. Though an honorable man, he did not have his father's skill. He could not handle the many people, such as General Monk (one of Cromwell's most successful soldiers) or Penn and Venables, who were plotting against him to restore the monarchy. The English public were tired of Puritan rule and military dictatorship and, forgetful of the Stuart family's arrogant attitude toward Parliament, were anxious to be ruled once more by a king. Charles II was brought over from Holland by the Navy, which was once again Royal in name and sympathies. Admiral Penn and Samuel Pepys, Secretary of the Admiralty, the man who wrote the now famous secret diaries, were among the leaders who went to fetch the King.

News of the restoration of the English monarchy reached Jamaica in August, 1660. Immediately Colonel D'Oyley had a rebellion on his hands. This was led by Colonel Tyson, who had recently caused Ysassi to flee, and Colonel Raymond. D'Oyley managed to put down the rebellion, created by men who questioned his power, but he became bewildered about his authority. He sent letters to London requesting instructions and asking who ruled Jamaica now that Charles II occupied the throne. The English in Jamaica believed that Charles had promised to return Jamaica to Spain in return for the Spanish King's help in regaining England. (Their fear may have been justified, but since the Spanish actually gave Charles no help, he felt no need to honor his promise.)

Almost a year passed before D'Oyley received a commission as governor of Jamaica and the new rank of general. He was also authorized to create a council. D'Oyley chose twelve men, all soldiers, and said about them that they were "a rough, self-seeking lot, not blessed with many scruples." D'Oyley was also empowered to give each common soldier ten acres of free land, but it was difficult to induce soldiers to settle down. Fighting and taking booty was so much easier and more profitable. Officers were given one thousand acres of free land, but these were not of much use to them since they had few slaves to work in the fields.

A census taken at this time showed that Jamaica had 2,458 men, 454 women, 44 children and 584 Negroes. D'Oyley saw to it that the Council was duly selected. Then, exhausted, he wrote to London begging to be relieved. He had come to Jamaica in 1655 with the original invading force, and now, after six years of alarms and troubles, he was anxious to see his home and family again. Miraculously, he had kept his health and held the struggling colony together.

Help did not arrive until August, 1662, when Lord Windsor came to relieve D'Oyley as governor. Sir Charles Lyttelton came at the same time to act as chancellor. He was the first such official to bring his wife.

Windsor's first act was to proclaim that the name of the new town, Port Royal, was official. He also published the King's proclamation that all children born of British subjects in Jamaica should be regarded as free citizens of England. A month after Windsor arrived, D'Oyley finally sailed for home.

Captain Mings, the Navy officer who had raided towns in Venezuela, had escaped punishment in England and returned to Port Royal. Shortly after D'Oyley left, Mings took his fleet on another excursion against the Spanish. They sailed to Santiago de Cuba, the second largest town on the island of Cuba. The spot Mings chose to land his men was very near the place where United States troops landed when they invaded Cuba a little more than two hundred years later, during the Spanish–American War.

Mings had eighteen ships and nine hundred men. The residents of Santiago scattered as the invaders approached. Resistance was minimal. The men from Jamaica held the town for five days, pillaging and plundering. In their rampage they destroyed two thousand houses and attacked a number of outlying plantations as well. They also blew up El Morro, the fort protecting the harbor, after stealing all the lighter guns. Having taken everything valuable that Santiago possessed, they left the ruins to the Spaniards and returned to Port Royal to divide up the enormous booty. By law one fifteenth of all the proceeds went to the King and one tenth to the Lord High Admiral, who was the King's brother, the Duke of York. Consequently, although Mings was technically not a pirate, he acted as one as far as the Spanish were concerned, and they might reasonably have considered that the Stuarts were in partnership with pirates.

Although one might sympathize with the Spaniards for suffering attacks such as that on Santiago, they were hardly innocent of provoking the British. Not long before the raid on Santiago, Spaniards had beheaded Colonel Arundell and another British officer and paraded their heads on pikes through the Cuban town of Matanzas.

As governor of Jamaica, Windsor enjoyed greater powers than D'Oyley. Windsor was told to take 400,000 acres, 100,000 in each quarter of the island, as the personal property of the King, perhaps to prove that His Majesty had no intention of returning Jamaica to Spain. Windsor was also to take 50,000 acres of land for himself. He was given the power to commission privateers. He called in all previous commissions—some issued by D'Oyley, some forgeries—and issued new ones in his own name. Among the new commissions was one given in 1662 to a Captain Henry Morgan. This is the first time the name of the famous buccaneer appears on any record.

Windsor expanded the number of privateers and gave them new official government respectability. Encouraging privateers had its drawbacks, however. A secure colony needed settled planters who were tied to their lands and anxious to have security —not fighters who were always sailing away to plunder the Spanish.

From the beginning, Jamaica had suffered because people could not be enticed into becoming planters. A man might make in an hour with his sword what he might not make in a year on a plantation. D'Oyley had reported that the climate was too unhealthy for a white man to want to work in it. And why should he? Though white indentured servants were legally bound to a master for a period of years, escape was easy. Arriving ships always needed new members for their crews, and escapees were signed on with no questions asked. Landowners feared the coming of a ship, for it meant they might lose hands needed to bring in a ripening crop.

Labor also became scarce whenever large forces were recruited for raids such as those against Santiago and Campeche. Many a debtor escaped from bondage by joining such expeditions. Many Jamaican debtors, and debtors from Barbados who managed to get themselves to Jamaica, eventually found their way to Virginia.

Lord Windsor did try to encourage planting, however. He proclaimed that "thirty acres of improveable land [would] be granted and allotted" to every person twelve years old or older, male or female, who resided in Jamaica. This was the basis for the great estates that soon grew up. A man with a few children over twelve years was given a good start. Often he could add to his holdings by purchasing the holdings of others who had failed as planters for one reason or another.

During Lord Windsor's brief rule, Jamaica's government changed from a military to a civil one. The new rule was by law rather than court-martial. Windsor disbanded the standing army and established a militia. He appointed a new Council to guide him. He had the power to organize an elected assembly, but he did not do this, because he had no desire to be bothered by a contentious little parliament.

Windsor had orders to take the buccaneer island of Tortuga, now under French governorship, but this was not carried out. Windsor governed in a hurry. He left Jamaica after ruling for only ten weeks. Officially he was supposed to be ill, but Samuel Pepys, in his diary, said that Windsor was simply too lazy for the work.

Captain Mings also returned to England about the same time.

From there he was to go to West Africa to fight the Dutch. The Dutch held a monopoly of the slave trade, and these particular hostilities began in order to break it up. The English had just formed the African Company for this purpose. The company had contracted to provide three hundred slaves a year to Jamaica. Without African slaves the plantations in America would never thrive.

On departing, Windsor had named Chancellor Lyttelton deputy governor. Lyttelton had begun his career as a soldier, a Cavalier, while still a very young man. His family lineage could be traced back to the twelfth century. Lyttelton's ancestors had served many kings personally, and he was profoundly Royalist. At the age of eighteen, after fighting at the siege of the small town of Colchester, a battle won by Cromwell's forces, he had escaped to France. There he became cupbearer to Charles II. Returning to England at the age of thirty to battle against the Lord Protector, he was captured, then set free. He rejoined Charles in Holland and engaged in the negotiations for the Stuart King's return to the throne. The appointment as deputy governor of Jamaica was his reward.

Lyttelton and Henry Morgan must have met, because the Deputy Governor approved Morgan's commission. Morgan was probably more often at Port Royal than at Tortuga now, and Lyttelton lived in the small town in the newly built King's House. Unfortunately, no record of any encounter between them exists. It would be interesting to have some picture of the great buccaneer at this early date. Morgan could and did write vivid letters when he had to, but, as much as possible, he did not commit himself to paper. Nor did he ever speak about himself if he didn't have to.

Lyttelton, on the other hand, and his wife wrote a number of letters which have been preserved and which reveal their unhappy circumstances in Jamaica. The new Deputy Governor had been married just before he was knighted and ordered to the West Indies.

His wife, a member of the minor nobility, was not in good

health. Before they left England her husband wrote to a friend, Lord Hatton: "My poor wife has been, as it were by a miracle, raised twice to life with Sir Walter Raleigh's cordial, when given over by her physicians and all her friends, and is now, thank God, in a probable way to recover."

A month after arriving in Jamaica, Lady Lyttelton also wrote to Lord Hatton.

Jamaica
Sept. 3rd, 1662

DEAR FRIEND,

I thought I should not be able to write a word to you, which was a great trouble to me, for I am very weak, and accidentally I began other letters before yours, and, by that time they were done, I was so ill I was not able to write another; but, now the ships [returning to England] are stayed longer than I thought, I have recovered a little strength to tell you I am alive, though not all well, being troubled with the symptoms and pains of a consumption, which I feared before I went from England. . . . I know not whether Charles be able to write to you, for he is very ill; but I hope the worst is past with him; but the disease of the country, which is a griping of the guts, has made him very weak. . . . Our greatest want is good company; but I am so dull, with being continually sick, that I think I could hardly divert myself with anything. . . .

Lady Lyttelton concluded her letter by saying, "The truth is, I can say no more of anything for I am already so weary I know not what to do." She died a few months later, in January, and her infant son followed her in five days. Both were buried in Spanish Town. It is hard to realize now how brief life spans were in that era.

In spite of his grief, Sir Charles carried on as best he could. Rather irrationally, he wrote to Lord Hatton about his hate for Lord Windsor, who, he said, had shown "inhumane discourtesy" to his wife. She might have been "a healthful and truly a happy woman" if this could have been prevented. Just what Lord Windsor did or said to Lady Lyttelton has never been explained.

The marauding against Spanish territory continued and Port Royal prospered. Very shortly after Lady Lyttelton died in 1663 an expedition sailed for Campeche, on the Yucatán Peninsula of Mexico. Henry Morgan and his crew took part in the raid. The Spaniards opposed the attack with vigor, but in the end the English won out and returned to Jamaica with much booty and numerous ships. Lyttelton, whose pay was in arrears, a not uncommon situation for colonial governors, took the thousand pounds due him out of the King's share from the Campeche raid and at the same time wrote to London asking to be relieved of his post. The buccaneers working out of Port Royal might be prospering, but it was an unhappy place for an officer of the Crown working on a salary in a climate that was very dangerous for Englishmen.

When King Charles heard about the raid on Campeche, he quickly told the Spanish ambassador, the Duke of Medina, that he disapproved of the action. Medina did not believe the King, but there was little he could do. At about this time British troops, fighting alongside Portuguese soldiers, defeated the Spanish in a battle near the Portuguese–Spanish border. Yet the English had not declared war against Spain. Medina decided that Spain should allow England, France and Holland to trade in Spanish ports. He hoped that this gesture might discourage piracy and ensure that no more Spanish islands would be taken, but his government did not agree with him and no action was taken.

Charles may have enjoyed seeing Spain suffer defeats, and he undoubtedly appreciated the wealth which privateering brought to him personally. He also wanted to do business with Spain. Thus, in July, he wrote to Lyttelton that, while he admired the dash of Mings's expedition to Cuba, such things really should cease. They interfered with planting, which, in the long run, would be more profitable.

The King did not actually order Lyttelton to outlaw privateering, however, and he even told Lyttelton to make sure that the King and the Duke of York received their just dues from the privateers' take. It seemed to be expected that privateering would continue, and so the bewildered Lyttelton did nothing about the situation.

In October, 1663, Lyttelton sent a report to London saying that the fortifications at Port Royal were only half finished and that costs were increasing. The food supply was better and prices were lower, he said, but only two hundred new settlers had arrived that year. There was still too much privateering and too much sickness. Settlers calling at Barbados were being discouraged from coming to Jamaica, because of the lack of labor there.

Again Lyttelton asked to be relieved of his post. He said that the island needed a man who wanted a career in the West Indies, not one who was always yearning for London. The governor should be a planter and an active man eager to encourage this island's growth. He himself was not such a man. He would like to show his loyalty to His Majesty in person. The widowed man was finally granted permission to go home in May, 1664.

Modyford's Personal War

Jamaica and the growing town of Port Royal began to know some lively days after Lyttelton's departure. The King followed Lyttelton's advice about the kind of governor the island needed, and named to the post Thomas Modyford, a cousin of Cromwell's General Monk, the same General Monk who stage-managed the Restoration. At the time of the Stuart return, Modyford was a wealthy planter in Barbados, and he had also been that island's governor. Barbados' politics were always turbulent, often violent, and Modyford and his numerous family had many feuds with other factions. [In addition, the elected Assembly showed signs of being very independent of England. It was here that the cry of the American Revolution, "No taxation without representation," had first been raised. Barbados was not so independent, though, that it failed to offer its allegiance to the new King.]

47

In spite of his extensive land holdings in Barbados, Modyford was enthusiastic when Charles offered him the governorship of Jamaica. He sent a number of proposals to London about how the government should be run. The island should prosper, he said, if decently planted, and there were a number of small landowners in Barbados and other Leeward Islands who could be induced to make the move, since these islands were all overcrowded. Modyford asked that the first thousand new settlers be given free passage to Jamaica. They should also be free men who could vote in the House of Assembly which Modyford planned to set up. Civil liberties should be announced for the island and also a twenty-one-year period when there would be no duty on trade. Privateers should be eliminated.

His ideas were liked by the King, and Modyford received the commission of governor of Jamaica in February, 1664. He was given the right to make laws, with the consent of the Assembly. He was to stop the commissioning of privateers. He also had the "power to act in all things not mentioned in these Instructions." That clause gave him considerable power.

In April, Lieutenant Colonel Sir Edward Morgan, who was to be deputy governor, arrived from England with three thousand pounds to run the government in Jamaica. This displeased Governor Willoughby of Barbados, who was jealous that the other island was being helped and considered it good only as a place from which to annoy the Spanish.*

Modyford was known to be intelligent, and the fact that he was leaving so much behind to establish himself in Jamaica did encourage many small planters to follow his example. When Modyford sailed from Barbados 987 settlers went with him, and not one

*The following year Willoughby was accused by his Assembly of embezzling the liquor duty and prize money, of falsifying his expense account, of disregarding (for his friends) the laws demanding that all trade be in British ships, of making unlawful imprisonments, of being disrespectful of the King, and of liking Jews.

of them was a fleeing debtor. Each would receive thirty acres free in the new land.

Modyford arrived at Port Royal with the new settlers on June 4. Immediately there were a number of matters to be attended to. In 1661 forty tavern licenses had been issued for the town of Port Royal alone. The principal drink was "rumbullion," or rum, distilled from the locally grown sugar cane. Liquor at the time was not highly refined, and the rum produced was raw and powerful. As happened during the days of Prohibition in the United States, many concoctions using sugar and various fruits were invented to disguise the taste of the rum. The buccaneers were thirsty when they returned after months at sea, and the water at Port Royal was bad. The result was such that the first elected Assembly, which met in 1664, passed a law against "tippling, cursing and swearing." As one might expect, this legislation had no effect whatsoever. When the second Assembly met later in the year, the elected members quarreled bitterly with Modyford's appointed Council. At the end of the session a party was held "to cement the rents that had been made." Assembly, Council and Governor met in a gay atmosphere livened by music, wine and rum. There was much "tippling," and the disagreements between the groups were more and more difficult to conceal. Then "honest Captain Ritter of the Assembly was killed by his friend, Major Ivy, of the Council." The affair ended in disorder. Major Ivy was never punished for the murder. The source of the argument was the desire of the Assembly to keep the King's name off bills concerning taxation. Like colonists elsewhere, they believed that control of taxation was their right alone. As soon as he could, Modyford dissolved the Assembly, and he never called it again while he remained governor.

Modyford did try to improve the financial condition of the island and sometimes to carry out the orders of the King concerning privateers. He introduced a much superior stock of sugar cane, one that he had grown in Barbados, and this soon improved the yield from the plantations. He also tried to seize a prize brought in by a Captain Searle, a Spanish ship, but the captain managed to escape him and sail away. Later Modyford sent a Captain Ensor to arrest a Captain Munro who had "turned pirate" and was capturing English ships. After a fierce fight Modyford's men did succeed in overwhelming the British pirates, who were brought to Port Royal. At a point overlooking the entrance to the harbor, where all passing ships could see them, the pirates were hung from poles and held by chains, their feet off the ground, until they died from thirst or the terrible heat of the sun.

This same year, however, Captain Maurice Williams, a buccaneer, went out and brought in a great prize of logwood (much in demand as a source of dye for cloth), indigo and silver. Bernard Nicholas also came in with a rich prize. There was no official reprisal for these acts. One can hardly blame the buccaneers if they were confused about their situation. When were they acting legally and when were they not?

In addition to these domestic problems, Modyford had the Dutch to contend with. In March of 1664 King Charles had given his brother, the Duke of York, all of North America between the Connecticut and Delaware Rivers. The central part of this gift, what is now New York, was in Dutch hands, so His Majesty gave the Duke four frigates to make good on this present. The frigates and their crew arrived at New Amsterdam on August 18 (though not with the Duke). Peter Stuyvesant reluctantly surrendered to the English when his outnumbered people would not fight. The following year, in March, the English finally declared war against Holland, and, a month later, Modyford organized an expedition against three of Holland's island strongholds in the West Indies.

Lieutenant Colonel Sir Edward Morgan, Modyford's deputy governor, was put in charge. This Morgan, along with his brother, Thomas, had been a mercenary in the Netherlands, fighting both for and against that country. The two brothers had been knighted by the Cromwells (how did a Commonwealth manage to create knighthoods?), but they managed to retain status after the Restoration. Sir Edward Morgan was an uncle of the mysterious Henry Morgan, but records make no mention of the fact until a later date. Perhaps they never encountered each other while in Jamaica. While Sir Edward Morgan was second in command there, Henry Morgan was busy, at least most of the time, in the Yucatán Peninsula.

On April 15, 1665, Sir Edward sailed with ten ships and 650 men against the Dutch islands of St. Eustatius, Saba and Curaçao, the last-named being the strongest outpost. Modyford, to ensure the element of surprise, dared not write to London about the matter until Morgan was well under way. Then he explained that the troops were all reformed privateers and that he was not denuding Jamaica of hard-working planters.

Sir Edward died very soon after the landing at St. Eustatius. Colonel Theodore Cary reported, "The Lieutenant General died, not with any wound, but being ancient and corpulent, by hard marching and extraordinary heat, fell and died, and I took command of the party by the desire of all."

Nevertheless, St. Eustatius was taken, along with cannon, small arms, livestock and 942 slaves. Over three hundred Dutch inhabitants were deported. The English expedition went on to capture the island of Saba. Then the privateers deserted, looking for an easier target than well-defended Curaçao. Cary and his officers had to return to Jamaica with their mission incomplete. The privateers went on to capture Tobago, only a few miles from Trinidad. When Lord Willoughby, Governor of Barbados, a thoroughly disliked man, claimed that these islands should rightly be his, the privateers suddenly claimed that they were acting for Modyford. Neither discipline nor patriotism was very strong in those years, and men changed their allegiance readily to take advantage of a given situation. What united men was hope of personal gain and hatred of the Spaniards. (Attacks on the Dutch and the French were not nearly so popular, though recruits could always be found if the rewards seemed sufficiently promising.)

Meanwhile, privateering continued out of Port Royal. Either Modyford could not prevent it or he did not care to. In September, 1665, Captains Henry Morgan and John Morris and a Captain Jackman returned from extended raids along the coast of Mexico. Governor Modyford wrote a long defense of their actions to London.

Twenty-two months before (said Modyford), not knowing that hostilities between England and Spain had ended, the men had set out for the Tabasco River—which empties into the Bay of Campeche—under a commission from Lord Windsor, then governor of Jamaica. Coming ashore at the river mouth, 107 men, guided by friendly Indians, had marched three hundred miles over tracks unknown to the Spanish and surprised the town of Villahermosa. This they took and plundered, capturing three hundred prisoners. On returning to their anchorage, they found that the Spanish had stolen their ships. The Spanish, waiting for them at sea, soon attacked the privateers, but were driven off without capturing or killing a single man.

The privateers' ships were gone, however. Therefore they built two small sailing ships and four canoes and went on to capture the little settlement of Río Carta. Then they crossed the broad Gulf of Honduras and took the rather populous town of Truxillo, principal port of the area, and captured a ship. Next they sailed to the Mosquito Cays, where they enlisted some Indians hostile to the Spanish. Returning to the mainland, they anchored in Monkey Bay near the Nicaragua River, up which they canoed. After traveling sixty or seventy miles and portaging around three waterfalls, they came upon large Lake Nicaragua. They found this bordered by excellent pasture land.

Rowing all night, guided by the Indians, hiding among the islands by day, the privateers landed in the dark, marched unnoticed into the center of the large town of Granada, and fired a volley to frighten the sleeping citizens. Then the invaders quickly overturned eighteen great guns in the central square, seized the sergeant major's house, which contained all the arms and ammunition, imprisoned in the church three hundred of the most able-bodied residents, and plundered the town for sixteen hours. Then they freed the prisoners, sank all the boats belonging to Granada, and sailed away. About a thousand Indians helped in the plundering and, thinking the English would remain, would have killed the prisoners. When they discovered that the English were leaving, the Indians asked them to return. They showed the privateers where there were better routes from the Caribbean to Lake Nicaragua and named a number of towns worth raiding. One of the towns they mentioned was El Realejo, on the Pacific, where the ships for commerce between Peru and Panama were built.

Modyford concluded his report by saying that perhaps as few as five hundred Englishmen could take this whole area. "If ever reasons of state at home require any attempt on the Spanish Indies, this is the properest place and the most probable to lay a foundation for the conquest of the whole."

The Governor was balancing on a very difficult tightrope. The government in England was openly at war with Holland and France. Spain clearly favored the Dutch cause, but England hoped the Spanish could be kept out of the conflict. Spanish warships in the Caribbean took English ships and treated the crews as pirates. The Spanish continued to demand the return of Jamaica and held great numbers of Englishmen captive, in Spain as well as in the West Indies, and these men were demanding to be liberated.

In spite of his own anti-Spanish sentiments, Modyford tried to follow the shifting policy of London. That policy might change from appeasing the Spanish one day to attacking them on the next, but Modyford might not hear about the changes for a number of months.

At the moment, the war with the Dutch was England's greatest concern. Though people did not generally realize it at the time, this was actually a battle for commercial supremacy of the world. Although the English in the West Indies had no great quarrel with the Dutch, Modyford continued to do what he could to wage war against them. Learning that the privateers planned another raid against Cuba, he sent a senior officer along with other privateer ships to persuade them to give up that venture and attack Dutch Curaçao instead. The officer returned without having found the privateers. He wrote in his diary that Admiral Mandevelt, who had been elected to that office by the Brethren of the Coast, would not sail against Curaçao and cared for dealing with no enemy except the Spaniards.

The position of Port Royal and Jamaica was not strong. The army had long been disbanded, and the Royal Navy had been withdrawn across the Atlantic years before to fight the Dutch. The only fighting ships in Jamaica belonged to the privateers, who, if ordered not to attack the Spanish, might easily return to Tortuga. The government there, now French, was freely handing out privateering commissions. The privateers could quite easily decide to sack Port Royal, since they knew well enough how defenseless it would be without them. Many of the buccaneers had already strayed from Jamaica and had attacked Cuba several times without benefit of any English authority.

When Modyford learned that many merchants were leaving Port Royal because privateers were departing, and that the town guard, which had numbered six hundred men a few years before, had dwindled to 130, he called together his Council so that arrangements for bringing in new recruits for the town guard from other parts of the island could be made. The Council members replied that the only way to fill Port Royal with men was to grant privateers commissions against the Spaniards. They felt very strongly about their case. After making certain that he had the Council's opinion in writing, Modyford consented. The decision to create new commissions for privateers was proclaimed, with the beat of a drum, through the streets of Port Royal in February, 1666.

The Council had prepared a resolution, for the benefit of the powers in London, stating their reasons for actively encouraging the buccaneers. The buccaneers' raids would furnish the island with many necessary commodities at easy rates, they said. Replenishing the island with coin, bullion, logwood, hides, tallow, indigo and many other commodities would entice men from New England to come to Jamaica to trade and would encourage many merchants to settle at Port Royal. It would help the slave trade. A prosperous port would also attract many settlers who would become planters. It was the only means to keep the buccaneers "on Hispaniola [Santo Domingo], Tortuga, and the South and North Quays [Cays] of Cuba" from becoming enemies of the English and attacking their plantations. Also, privateers often obtained useful intelligence of Spanish actions. Their booty helped enrich the King and the Duke of York. They provided work at high wages for many skilled men. Their existence helped frighten the Spanish. Finally, the Council said, desisting from granting new commissions had done nothing to curb the ferocity of the Spaniards. "It was unanimously concluded that the granting of said commissions did extraordinarily conduce to the strengthening, preservation, enriching, and advancing the settlement of this island."

With the consent of his Council, then, the Governor of Jamaica had in effect declared his own personal war against Spain. He had also provided a legal setting for Henry Morgan's extraordinary career.

Sʳ HEN MORGAN

Part. 2 Page. 60

THE BETTMANN ARCHIVE, INC.

The Extraordinary Career of Henry Morgan Begins

There is nothing moral about history, and few morals can be learned from it. History is full of stories about people or groups who claimed superior virtue—religious sects, abolitionists, prohibitionists, patriots of every hue—and caused more woe, more bloodshed, more sorrow than any self-admitted criminal. The Thirty Years' War, which ended only seven years before England conquered Jamaica almost bloodlessly, was fought in the name of religion, Protestant against Catholic faith. Different interpretations of the message of Jesus Christ caused the death of many millions of people. More murders have been caused in the name of righteousness than for any other reason.

There have always been people and groups who believed they had a right to impose their opinions on others by force (Communists, Fascists, various religions and nationalist groups, for instance). Many writers have called Henry Morgan a criminal, a pirate, an inhuman and beastly man. In fact he was a man who behaved in the custom of his time. The difference between Morgan and many other men long forgotten is that when it came to attacking and looting cities, Morgan was supremely successful. He seems to have had no other particular virtue.

The seventeenth century, which might be associated loosely with names like the royal house of Stuart and Louis XIV, was a high-water mark in the story of hypocrisy. Men wrote with exquisite courtliness, and behaved with a beastliness greater than any animal in the jungle. The most outrageous conduct in that century, whether between individuals or nations, was always clothed in a blanket of self-righteous decency. A man like Henry Morgan seldom bothered with such fictions. He did not like to talk about himself or his success. No doubt that is why he is such a problem for writers who want to draw morals or merely to gossip. Henry Morgan, in life, never let any human defeat him. Neither will any historian.

Henry Morgan was born in Wales. Until his name appears in the records of Jamaica as a privateer commissioned in 1662, this is the only certain fact about him. He has been described as very dark, not tall, quite strong, and agile as a cat. In order to survive in Jamaica, where the death rate among the first English settlers from disease was extraordinarily high, and to live through his quite arduous campaigns against the Spanish, Morgan must have been a very tough man.

Writers about him have sought to discover something about his family and the date of his birth, but they have uncovered nothing. That he had two uncles who were knighted is known, but his own father's name is not. Morgan's father was probably a farmer but also a gentleman, which means that he could vote. Morgan was literate, and most members of the lower classes were not. In one of the rare moments when he spoke about himself, during the conduct of a lawsuit, he indicated that he was born in 1635, which would have made him twenty-seven years old when his name first appeared on any document.

How he came to the West Indies is not known. A frequently repeated story is that as a boy he was kidnapped in the Welsh seaport town of Cardiff, then transported to Barbados, where he served for some years as an indentured servant on a plantation. Many years later, when Morgan had become famous, a book about pirates appeared, written in Dutch, that repeated this story about his youth. The author, who signed himself "Esquemelin," also claimed that Morgan permitted his men to be very barbarous, that he cheated them out of the booty they had earned and that he once even abandoned them. When two London booksellers published translations of Esquemelin's book, Morgan sued them for libel and succeeded in winning damages and printed retractions. In an affidavit he said that he had "the greatest abhorence and distrust" of "evil deeds, piracies and robberies," and that "for the kind of men called buccaneers he always had and still has hatred." As to having been an indentured servant in Barbados, he added, "I have never been a servant to any man except, perhaps, to the King." He also wrote, about this time, "I left the schools too young to be a great proficient in laws, and have been much more used to the pike than the book."

Morgan never did explain what he had been doing in the years before he appeared in Port Royal at the age of twenty-seven. He must have been well known to the buccaneers of Tortuga, because in 1666, when Admiral Mandevelt of the Brethren set out on an expedition against Providence Island, he named Morgan as his vice-admiral. Providence Island, a small island off the coast of Central America, had been settled for many years by English Puritans. But the Spaniards had occupied it, after ferociously wiping out the settled population. Mandevelt and his troops attacked the Spanish in retaliation and drove them from Providence. Then the buccaneers went into Nicaragua and sacked the large town of Granada.

Some time after his return to Port Royal from this expedition Morgan married his first cousin Mary Elizabeth. She was the second daughter of the Sir Edward Morgan who had died of a heart attack while fighting the Dutch on St. Eustatius. In spite of his titles and position, Sir Edward had left his six children almost penniless. The date of the marriage between the two cousins is not known, because the marriage records at Port Royal were lost. Mary Elizabeth's older sister had married Major Robert Byndloss, a member of the House of Assembly and owner of two thousand acres of land. Morgan and Byndloss became friends. Morgan began to buy land himself and also acquired a house in Port Royal. He also became friends with the Governor, Sir Thomas Modyford, and it might have seemed that he was on his way to becoming a respectable citizen.

This was not quite the case, however. When Mandevelt died, the Brethren elected Morgan their admiral, no doubt because of the success he had already had as a privateer. Then, early in 1668, Modyford, with the advice of his Council, issued a special commission to Morgan naming him a colonel. Morgan was ordered "to draw together the English privateers and take prisoners of the Spanish nation, whereby you may gain information of that enemy [of their plans] to attack Jamaica, of which I have had frequent and strong advice." Reportedly the commission also restricted Morgan to attacking Spanish ships at sea, but the original document disappeared, a fact that Morgan must have appreciated.

Morgan soon assembled ten ships and some five hundred men, most of them veterans of other raids. The fleet sailed from Port Royal to the Isle of Pines, just south of Cuba and not too distant from Havana. The residents of Havana had been expecting a British or French attack for some time and, led by an energetic bishop, had greatly strengthened the city's defenses.

The captains of the ships in Morgan's flotilla met to consider their best move. They decided to bypass Havana and attack the inland town of Puerto Principe instead. Next to Havana, Puerto Principe was believed to be the wealthiest town in Cuba. It had grown rich on trade in hides and cattle. Captain Hadsell, one of the men at the meeting, had been a prisoner in Cuba and, while escaping, had learned a good deal about the Cuban countryside. He and others who had been prisoners in Cuba were anxious for revenge.

There are numerous small islands along the south coast of Cuba that were well known to the buccaneers as places to hide and also to find many turtles and wild fowl for food. Morgan concealed his ships among these islands, leaving a few sick men to guard them. With the rest of the crew he landed at night on Cuban soil at the Bay of Ana María. They marched more than thirty miles over rough and mountainous country in not much more than twenty-four hours. They failed to surprise the town of Puerto Principe, however, because a Cuban they had captured and used as a guide had escaped in the dark and raised the alarm. As they descended a hill outside the town, the privateers were met by the mayor, with seven hundred men on foot and one hundred more on mules and ponies. The Cubans were brave enough but absolutely untrained. They made a wild rush against the invaders and were met by careful, well-aimed musket fire. The mayor and several of his men were killed. The others fled. Undaunted by this disaster, the people fought the privateers from the roof tops as they entered the town. More than one hundred of the Spaniards were killed and many more taken prisoner before the English finally drove the inhabitants out of the town. Then they looted the houses, looking for anything valuable that could be taken away.

A deputation of Spaniards soon came. They wanted to offer to ransom the town before the invaders decided to burn it down. Morgan set the ransom as a large number of cattle.

In his official report, Morgan described the attack on Puerto Principe as a preventive measure taken for the safety of Jamaica:

We were driven to the south keys of Cuba where, being like to starve, and finding French in like condition, we put our men ashore, and finding all the cattle driven up country and the inhabitants fled, we marched 20 leagues to Porto Principe on the north of the island, and with little resistance possessed ourselves of the same. There we found that 70 men had been pressed to go against Jamaica; that the like levy had been made in all the island, and considerable forces were expected from Vera Cruz and Campeche to rendezvous at Havana and from Porto Bello and Cartagena to rendezvous at Santiago of Cuba, of which I immediately gave notice to Governor Modyford. On the Spaniard's entreaty we forbore to fire the town, or bring away prisoners, but on delivery of 1,000 beefs, released them all.

Perhaps the Spanish were planning to attack Jamaica, but Morgan did not immediately return to defend it. He decided instead to visit Puerto Bello, a strongly fortified town near today's Panama Canal. First, however, he and his men spent a month among the Cuban islands, doing work on the ships, killing cattle and curing the meat for the long trip ahead.

For forty days out of the year Puerto Bello was probably the most tempting target in the Caribbean. This was the time of the town's annual fair, when merchant ships from Spain arrived carrying European goods to sell to the wealthy Spanish colonists who lived in the Pacific provinces. After unloading their cargo the ships would pick up all the gold, silver, emeralds and pearls that had been produced in the provinces during the year.

Puerto Bello was a vastly unhealthy place, surrounded by swamps. It was so deadly for white men that the Spanish, not noted in those days for their compassion, relieved the troops in the town's forts every three months. Puerto Bello was deserted during most of the year, but, in spite of the risk of disease, it was crowded during the time of the fair. The harbor was very large, but could be entered only by a narrow channel dominated on either side by a large castle. Another large fortress stood over the harbor itself. In 1596 Sir Francis Drake had sailed past the harbor, trying to decide how he could force his way in. He died there without having found the answer. Now, after much more work had been done on the defenses, Puerto Bello was considered impregnable.

Henry Morgan did not think this was true. He decided to land some one hundred miles away on the coast and approach the town in canoes. The French privateers he had with him did not like this idea and decided to leave him.

This is Morgan's official report of the attack on Puerto Bello:

Setting sail in May last we fell in with the coast of Puerto Bello and being informed of levies made there also against Jamaica and also by some prisoners who had made their escape from Providence that divers Englishmen were kept in irons in the dungeon of the castle of the town, we thought it our duty to attempt that place.

The French wholly refused to join in an action so full of danger; so leaving our ships on June 26, forty leagues to leeward at Bogota, we took our canoes, twenty-three in number, and rowing along the coast, landed at three o'clock in the morning and made our way into the town, and seeing that we could not refresh ourselves in quiet we were enforced to assault the castle, which we took by storm, and found well supplied with ammunition and provisions, only undermanned, being about 130 men, whereof 74 were killed...

In the dungeon we found eleven English in chains who had been there two years . . . [We] were informed . . . that the Prince of Monte Circa had been there with orders from the King of Spain to raise 2,200 men against us out of the Province of Panama, which Puerto Bello stands in, the certainty whereof was confirmed by all the Grandees [Spanish noblemen].

The Governor of the second castle refusing to permit our ships free entrance into the port, we were forced to attempt the taking of it, which ended in the delivering up the castle and marching out with colors flying, and the third castle immediately surrendered to five or six Englishmen.

And now having possession of the town and three castles, in the former were 900 men that bare arms, the fifth day arrived the President of Panama, with about 3,000 men; whom we beat off with considerable damage, in so much that the next day he proffered 100,000 pieces of eight for delivery of the town and castles in as good condition as we found them. . . .

We further declare to the world that in all this service of Puerto Bello, we lost but eighteen men killed and thirty-two wounded, and kept possession of the place thirty-one days; and for the better vindication of ourselves against the usual scandals of that enemy, we aver that having several ladies of great quality and other prisoners, they were proffered their liberty to go to the President's camp, but they refused, saying they were now prisoners to a person of quality, who was more tender of their honours than they doubted to find in the President's camp among his rude Panama soldiers, and so voluntarily continued with us until the surrender of the town and castles, when with many thanks and good wishes they repaired to their former homes.

As Morgan expected, he and his men were accused of "scandals" for their attack on Puerto Bello. Other accounts said that he used nuns and priests as hostages during the fighting, that his men murdered, tortured and raped, and then laughed at their victims.

Morgan and his men returned to Port Royal on the seventeenth day of August, 1668. The town gave Morgan a triumphal welcome. Four hundred privateers had stormed an impregnable, fortified city and left with 300,000 pieces of eight. It is not known whether Morgan ever mentioned to his wife "the ladies of great quality" he had charmed in Puerto Bello.

Modyford naturally worried about how the news of Morgan's latest exploits would be received in London. He wrote:

. . . the privateers have had the confidence to take two towns from the Spaniards, for which [they are] being reproved, having commissions only against their ships. . . . It is most certain that the Spaniards had full intention to attempt this island, but could not get men; and they still hold the same minds, and therefore I cannot but presume to say that it is very unequal that we should in any measure be restrained while they are at liberty to act as they please upon us, from which we shall never be secure until the King of Spain acknowledges this island to be his Majesty's and so includes it by name in the capitulations.

Two facts saved the Governor and Morgan from serious trouble at this time. The French had just created a very powerful fleet, which was sailing in the Caribbean under Admiral d'Estrées and plundering in Cuba and Santo Domingo. So far they had gone against the Spanish only, but there was no guarantee that they would always leave the increasingly wealthy town of Port Royal alone. The English government was too poor right then to give much help to its colony in Jamaica. In 1665 London had suffered greatly during the Great Plague. The following year the city was partially destroyed in a devastating fire. Such events of course had severe repercussions on the economy. The budget for the Navy had been cut drastically. The most support that London could manage for the island's defense was one fifth-rate frigate, the *Oxford*. The colony agreed to pay the crew and feed them. The ship arrived in October, 1668, and Modyford immediately put it under Morgan's command, as a privateer.

Modyford doubtless shared in the great profits from the raid on Puerto Bello, and soon he gave Morgan another commission against the Spanish. On January 2, 1669, Morgan was on board the *Oxford*, which was anchored near the Ile à Vache, off the south coast of Santo Domingo—either having a drinking bout, it has been said, or, as others have written, with his officers plotting an attack on the town of Cartagena—when the ship blew up, killing everybody on board but Morgan and the officers with him.

The accident did not deter Morgan. Instead of Cartagena, however, he decided to attack Maracaibo, on the coast of what is now Venezuela. This town had already suffered some years before at the hands of L'Ollonais, a French buccaneer with a reputation for being bloodthirsty. He had earned some of his ill fame at Maracaibo. Morgan may have thought this town had more wealth than Cartagena or was an easier target; or perhaps he felt challenged by the other leader's success.

The town of Maracaibo lies at the narrow, shallow entrance to an inland sea of the same name. Lake Maracaibo, more than one hundred miles long and seventy-five miles across at its widest point, is today one of the greatest oil fields in the world. In Morgan's time the town that controls it was a major trading port. Ever since the previous raid by L'Ollonais, "the fears which the Spaniards had conceived . . . were so great, that only hearing the leaves on the trees to stir, they often fancied them to be pirates."

When Morgan arrived with eight ships and five hundred men, a great number of citizens fled to the south and the buccaneers looted at will. Convinced that the refugees had taken much wealth with them, Morgan's fleet then sailed down Lake Maracaibo to the little town of Gibraltar, where they found many people from Maracaibo. It does seem that here the buccaneers tortured people to find out where treasures had been hidden. After extracting booty worth about 250,000 pieces of eight, the buccaneers embarked to return to Port Royal. At the entrance to the lake, however, they found their passage blocked by three men-of-war that had just come from Spain with the specific purpose of capturing or killing them.

Henry Morgan's fame came from the skill with which he led fighting forces on land, but on this occasion he showed himself equally resourceful as a sailor. Apparently trapped, he resorted to cunning. The Spanish ships seemed reluctant to attack, so Morgan had time to work. He had his men fill canoes with pitch and other inflammable material. Then he staged a fake attack against the fort at Maracaibo. When the Spanish ships sailed in to the rescue, Morgan launched his flaming canoes against them, and two of the Spanish ships caught on fire. The third was destroyed in shallow water by Morgan's guns. Morgan's men swarmed aboard this vessel and found it was carrying a considerable amount of silver. This was added to the rest of their booty. and the victorious buccaneers sailed free to their home port.

Meanwhile, policy toward Spain had changed again in England. Governor Modyford received orders to call in all commissions against the Spanish, and this he did as soon as Morgan returned from his recent successful raid. Modyford also wrote to all the Spanish governors telling them that their troubles, which had been caused by their inhuman treatment of the English, were now at an end. Then he wrote a very undiplomatic, sarcastic letter to the Count of Molina, Spanish ambassador in London:

> SIR,
>
> You cannot be ignorant how much your whole nation in these parts did applaud my justice and civility to them at my first coming to this government, which (notwithstanding the small return I received) I should have continued to this day, had not an invincible necessity compelled me to allow our privateers their old way, that I might keep them from joining mine and your Masters' enemies [the French] to which I find them much too inclinable. . . .
>
> I know and perhaps you are not altogether ignorant of your weakness in these parts, the thinness of your inhabitants, want of hearts, arms and knowledge in war, the open opposition of some and doubtful obedience of other of the Indians, so that you have no town on this side of the Line but that my master's forces would give him, did not his signal generosity to yours restrain them. What we could have done, the French will do, unless these men by your intercession be brought to serve your master, and then you will be so sensible of their usefulness that you will no longer malign me for the evils they have done the vassals of your prince. . . .

It would seem that Modyford was suggesting that the Spanish employ the very men who had been raiding and looting their towns. This seems like one of the strangest ideas of that strange time.

While Modyford was proclaiming peace between himself and the Spanish governors, the Queen of Spain, acting as regent for an infant King, was sending orders to these same governors to declare war against all English south of the Tropic of Cancer, with permission to seize all English ships. The Governor of Cartagena declared this war against the English in February, 1670, but Modyford did not know it until June, when Spaniards landed on both the north and south shores of Jamaica, burning many houses and taking prisoners. Modyford called for his privateers and on June 29 made Henry Morgan an admiral.

Morgan's order's were to "attack, seize and destroy all the enemy vessels that shall come within his reach . . . , to do and perform all manner of exploits which may tend to the preservation and quiet of Jamaica," and to divide the booty "according to their usual rules." This time Morgan finally received official permission to fight on land as well.

There may have been some sarcasm in these further instructions to Morgan:

> You are to inquire what usage our prisoners have had and what quarter has been given by the enemy to such of ours as have fallen under their power; and being well informed you are to give the same, or rather, as our custom is, to exceed them in civility and humanity, endeavouring by all means to make all sorts of people sensible of your moderation and good nature and your inaptitude and loathness to spill the blood of man.

It is hard not to believe that Sir Thomas thought he was being very funny.

In Madrid, only ten days after Modyford gave these orders to Morgan, Spain and England signed a treaty of peace. All past grievances were to be forgotten. Ships of either nation were to be free to enter the other's ports in case of distress (but not to trade there). And Spain recognized the English right to those lands in America that England already possessed. In fact this meant that Spain was finally giving up its claim to Jamaica, though the treaty did not name the island specifically.

Before this news could reach Port Royal (it took at least a month to reach Jamaica from Europe), Morgan had sailed in July to the Ile à Vache with twenty-eight English ships plus eight ships that had been captured from the French. While he rested on the island, considering his next major moves, his ships casually raided the coast of Cuba from time to time. And one of his captains took revenge for a Spanish insult.

In July a paper had been found nailed to a tree on the western end of Jamaica. In part it read:

> I, Captain Manuel Rivero Pardal, went on shore at Caimanos and burnt twenty houses, and fought with Captain Ary and took from him a catch laden with provisions and a canoe. And I am he who took Captain Baines, and did carry the prize to Cartagena, and am now arrived on this coast and burned it. And I come to seek Captain Morgan, with two ships of twenty guns, and I crave that, having seen this, he would come out upon the coast and seek me, that he might see the valor of the Spaniards. And because I had no time I did not come to the mouth of Port Royal to speak by word of mouth in the name of my King, whom God preserve.

Morgan was not one to bother with fighting duels. But Captain Morrice of his fleet found Pardal in a bay off Cuba and killed "the vaporing Admiral of St. Jago."

Morgan's fleet set off for Panama, the target Morgan had selected, the day before news of the peace arrived from Europe. Modyford immediately sent a ship to head Morgan off, but the ship could not find him, or at least so the Governor said. In fact Morgan kept his plans so much to himself that Modyford may not have known where he was going or where to look for him.

Morgan's force proceeded first to Providence Island, which the

Spanish had retaken, and proceeded to drive the Spanish out. Then they sailed on to the Chagres River and captured the Spanish fortifications there. They tried sailing up the river, but had to leave their ships and boats behind the next day. Morgan had twelve hundred men with him. They were tough and seasoned fighters, but no privateers had ever gone through the ordeals these men experienced before they won their prize.

Their goal, the city of Panama, on the Pacific side of the Isthmus, was one of the greatest cities in the New World. The Spanish conqueror Francisco Pizarro had built in Panama the ships on which he and his men sailed to conquer Peru in 1531, and he had brought back to Panama the treasure he found. For more than one hundred years the city had grown in wealth and power. Sir Francis Drake had raided it in 1572, but this was only a temporary setback in its prosperity. No one had molested the city since Drake, and it had become the home of peaceful merchants rather than the rugged soldiers who first settled it.

Panama had two thousand large houses made of cedar, many smaller ones, and numerous warehouses full of gold and silver, gems and pearls, waiting to be shipped back to Spain. The city had six churches, two convents and an imposing cathedral. The houses of religion were heavily decorated in gold and the vestments of the clergy ornamented with precious stones.

Morgan and his men had a good idea of all this, and perhaps that is why they were able to put up with their sufferings. Hoping, of course, to achieve surprise, Morgan had chosen, not the regular Spanish route across the Isthmus, but jungle trails, often through pestiferous swamps full of monkeys, mosquitos and snakes. Fevers were common, including the yellow fever that took so many lives two centuries later when a canal was being dug in this area. The buccaneers had brought hardly any food with them, expecting to live off the lush plantations that lay on the banks of the Chagres River. But they found no plantations, only dense green jungle. Sometimes they saw cattle tracks, but the live animals had been driven off as word came of the English advance. They saw some evidence of soldiers' camps, but the men had run away. Hope for a surprise attack had to be given up. The heat was almost as bad as the hunger, and many men felt like dropping in their tracks, particularly during the long climb over a small mountain range. Faith in Morgan, who had never failed, kept them going, as well as faith that he would lead them to unimagined heaps of gold.

Then, on the evening of the eighth day, they came to the brow of a hill and saw Panama spread out below them. One man saw a herd of cattle browsing a few hundred feet away and he ran toward the astonished beasts, shouting and waving his sword. More than a thousand famished men followed him, slaughtering and spilling blood. They ate the meat raw, still hot from the living animals. Then most of them slept.

In the early morning the buccaneers were awakened and Morgan gave them a talk before the battle. Morgan had had scouts out during the night. He warned his twelve hundred men that they were facing four thousand trained soldiers and that the defense had plans to loose bulls on them. Then he went on to inspire them by inciting their lust for women, for drink, for food and for plunder.

At this moment the Spanish cavalry began to advance. First they performed a number of very stylish maneuvers, with various formations. They started to charge. Then, incredibly, the whole troop rode right into a swamp, and horses and men fell in a hopeless confusion. Their commander had known the swamp was there, but in his excitement about the coming fight he had forgotten about it.

The Governor panicked for a moment (the cavalry leader had been his son), then remembered the plan about the bulls. He ordered them released from their pen, and, goaded with sharp picks, the great animals began to stampede toward the buccaneers. These men, who had lived by hunting wild cattle, took careful aim and fired as the beasts rushed toward them. The terrified animals stopped, smelled blood, saw this new danger in front of them, turned and ran wildly into the line of Spanish soldiers, who were all in orderly drill formation. The buccaneers ran right behind the bulls and followed where the bulls had crashed through the line. Then, swinging to the right and to the left, the buccaneers began slashing at the Spanish, who had never been trained for wild fighting like this. The savagery of the attack soon caused the Spaniards to bolt. Most of the defenders were killed, but some managed to escape into the jungles or the hills. Panama lay open to Morgan and his men.

There is hardly any doubt that the men acted savagely when they occupied the city. They behaved as conquerors always did, particularly when the enemy was Spanish and gold the great reward. No one knows how Panama caught fire (this was not a usual tactic of the buccaneers), but, in time, the fire raged so fiercely that the city was virtually destroyed—not, however, before Morgan and his men had removed vast amounts of booty from it.

Morgan's share of the treasure took 175 pack horses to transport across the Isthmus. The final estimate of the Spanish loss was six million crowns. No attempt was ever made to rebuild the ruined city. A new Panama was begun at another location.

When Morgan returned from Panama to Port Royal, he was given a triumph such as the Romans used to hold. He returned with only three ships, casually leaving the rest of his men to get back as best they could.

Meanwhile, having been unable or perhaps unwilling to stop Morgan from going to Panama, Modyford had written to London in self-defense. He said he had sent a message to Morgan to conduct the war with all possible moderation. Privateers would plunder, but did not soldiers also "look on the enemy as the surest pay?" Modyford believed that the Spanish were a menace and deserved what they got. If he had to do it again for the safety of Jamaica, he would do the same thing. Would His Majesty understand?

His Majesty would not. He revoked Modyford's commission, appointed Sir Thomas Lynch to be the new governor and gave

Lynch orders to arrest Modyford and send him home a prisoner. The charge was that Modyford had "contrary to the King's express commands made many depredations and hostilities against the subjects of His Majesty's good brother the Catholic King."

In fact, however, the King's "express commands" were never very clear. Modyford could show several orders that would have made an excellent defense of his behavior in a court of law. After the news from Panama, though, the King wanted to soothe the Spanish somewhat. Their Queen "was in such a distemper and excess of weeping and violent passion as those about her feared it might shorten her life." King Charles sent her a message that he would inflict a severe punishment fitting the seriousness of the crime. Meanwhile, till Modyford could be brought to London his son, Charles, would sit in the Tower in his place.

Lynch's orders were written in January, 1671, but he did not arrive in Jamaica until June 25. Then he feared to arrest Modyford. Not only did the dismissed Governor have four hundred slaves and servants, but Lynch believed that the privateers would rise to his defense. It took Lynch three months to find courage to make the arrest, and then he did it in such a cowardly way, while Modyford was a guest at his table, that it gave him a bad reputation right at the start of his administration.

Lynch had been instructed to tell Modyford, in private, after he was safely in custody, that he need not worry about his life or his fortune but that "there was a necessity of the King's making this resentment for such an unreasonable eruption." Lynch may have gone too far in his assurances in order to keep his prisoner quiet, because Modyford was indignant at being sent back to England as a prisoner and then put in the Tower in place of his son.

Modyford was obviously a man of intelligence, a strong character with a well-developed sense of his own rights. A successful planter in Barbados and Jamaica, he also saw that financial rewards often came with political power and he did not hesitate to take advantage of the fact. He made a number of enemies in both colonies, but also a number of powerful friends. In his letters and official reports, he betrayed a sense of humor as he punctiliously announced how he was carrying out the King's orders while at the same time scheming with Morgan and others to get around the law. That he connived at Morgan's raid on Panama seems obvious enough, but he evidently believed that the King would not actually mind at all. These were very cynical times and what a man said and what he did were entirely different matters. The worldly Governor Modyford considered that he was playing by the rules, and to be imprisoned just so the King could impress the Spanish seemed to him outside the rules as the game was then played. No wonder he was outraged.

The new Governor who succeeded him also had orders to send Henry Morgan to London, and this worried him even more. He was afraid that the privateers might think they all would be arrested, even though the King had sent a general proclamation of pardon. Lynch wrote to London that he would send Morgan home in such a way that the order would be obeyed and the Spaniards satisfied, but Morgan would not be disgusted. He could not send Morgan right away, however, because Morgan was sick and anyway no ships were available. "To speak the truth of him," Lynch wrote, "he's an honest brave fellow. . . . However, it must be confessed that the privateers did diverse barbarous acts, which they lay to his Vice-Admiral's charge."

Major General Banister, the new commander of the forces in Jamaica, also wrote to London about Morgan: "He is a well-deserving person, and one of great courage and conduct, who may, with his Majesty's pleasure, perform good public service at home or be very advantageous to this island if war should again break forth with the Spaniards."

With no great fear in his heart, Morgan finally sailed to England as a prisoner aboard the frigate *Welcome* in April, 1672. The Spanish were given the impression that he was lodged in the Tower immediately on arrival, but Morgan was seen frequently during the next year in London's taverns and theaters. No mention is made of the whereabouts of his wife.

Defiant Colonists

After the lively time of Modyford and Morgan, whose partnership had so enriched them, the privateering people of Port Royal found the governorship of Sir Thomas Lynch irritating and dull. Lynch ordered a survey of Jamaica made and good maps produced. He had a census taken and found that the population numbered 17,272. He complained that Port Royal was unhealthy, lacked streets and was so overcrowded that it could not even provide a good house for the King's minister. Fearing a Spanish invasion, Lynch made himself unpopular by declaring martial law and then permitting defensive measures only. (Morgan would naturally have protected the island by offensive action.)

Lynch was able to report that the slave trade flourished and that land had been found for all the immigrants who had recently arrived from Surinam (later Dutch Guiana)—British settlers who had been displaced when England traded Surinam to Holland in return for New York.

Under Lynch a problem involving the cutting of logwood became serious. This valuable commodity was used in the making of dyes, and it sold for high prices in Europe. It grew around Campeche on the Yucatán Peninsula, land claimed by the Spanish but not occupied by them. Men who were no longer employed as privateers found that cutting the logwood around Campeche was very lucrative. The Spanish considered such foresting piracy, so Lynch was instructed by London to permit it only in areas which were away from any Spanish settlements. Following out his orders, Lynch did not interfere with the harvesting of logwood, and this led to his downfall. He did not seem to realize that the orders were unofficial, and that while he could connive at the trade, it was not public policy. Once again the English government wanted to have it both ways. They would not admit that they had authorized their subjects to cut trees on Spanish soil, but they wanted the practice to continue. The Spanish ambassador in London was so outraged by the logwood affair that the government decided to dismiss the Governor of Jamaica. Lynch complained that the King had sacrificed "the only man who has resolutely obeyed His Majesty in these Indies."

Then the Spanish ambassador heard other rumors in London which worried him even more. He heard that Modyford, the man who had declared his own private war against Spain, would replace Governor Lynch. The actual fact, when it was learned, was almost as bad. Morgan was to become lieutenant governor. What is more, he had been knighted. Sir Henry Morgan! Such was Morgan's punishment for the sack of Panama.

What went on in London during the year and a half between Morgan's arrival as a prisoner and the time he received a title and the King's commission is not known. Neither he nor Modyford ever stood trial. Modyford had powerful friends and Morgan a great reputation, of course, as a man who could handle Spaniards.

Modyford had shown the English how to grow sugar successfully in Jamaica, and Morgan was the man who could command the privateers if they should be needed. Intrigue, no doubt, had something to do with the reversal of fortunes.

The King, when he appointed Morgan, wrote that he had "particular confidence in [Morgan's] loyalty, prudence, and courage, and long experience of that colony." That Sir Henry was prudent can hardly have been the King's reason for giving him the position.

Morgan was to be second in command to the new Governor, Lord Vaughan. That gentleman ordered Morgan to keep him company on the way to Port Royal. Morgan, however, somehow lost Lord Vaughan's ship at sea and sailed in his own ship, the *Jamaica Merchant*, to his old pirate haunt the Ile à Vache. The ship was wrecked there, but Morgan found another and arrived at Jamaica seven days before Vaughan. He took over from Lynch as acting governor and as such greeted the angry Vaughan when he finally arrived.

The King had once again forbidden privateers. But Morgan, whose new duties included being judge of legal matters to do with shipping, did what he could to help his old friends. He recommended the best of them to d'Ogeron, an old comrade who had become leader of the Brethren on Tortuga. They received French commissions as privateers, and Morgan received a substantial sum for the service he had performed. Privateering for England ended and the King of England thus lost a valuable source of revenues.

Morgan and his brother-in-law, Byndloss, were named to a committee which was ordered to examine the accounts of former Governor Lynch, who had returned to England. The committee soon accused Lynch of having sold gunpowder to the Spanish and cheating on the disposal of a prize ship full of Negro slaves.

The Jamaica Assembly voted Morgan six hundred pounds for his services to the colony, but Lord Vaughan resisted. He wrote London that he was very weary of Morgan, that Morgan should be recalled, and that, moreover, Morgan had cheapened himself drinking and gambling in the taverns of Port Royal. Vaughan also wrote, "I find Sir Henry, contrary to his duty and trust, endeavours to set up privateering, and has obstructed all my designs and purposes for the reducing of those that do use that course of life."

Vaughan issued proclamations calling in all privateers and forbidding Englishmen to accept such commissions from the French. He seems to have done these things without much conviction, however, since he wrote to London, ". . . these Indies are so vast and rich and this kind of rapine so sweet that it is one of the hardest things in the world to draw those from it who have used it for so long." He added, "Let His Majesty send what orders he will about privateering, there are almost none to execute them but who are in one way or the other interested [in privateering]."

In July, 1676, after about a year of quarreling, Vaughan brought charges of privateering against Sir Henry and Byndloss, dismissed Sir Henry as lieutenant governor, and removed both brothers-in-law from the Council. This brought Vaughan a rebuke from London, saying that the King was displeased that a governor should take it into his own hands to remove a man in whom His Majesty had placed his confidence.

At this juncture Lord Vaughan apparently gave up hope of stopping privateering. He began to engage in illicit trading himself, aided by the advice of Sir Thomas Modyford. When news of the Governor's behavior reached London, the authorities there started to look for a new man. They found him in the Earl of Carlisle.

Vaughan departed from Jamaica in March, 1678, and Morgan soon established himself as acting governor until Carlisle arrived. During this brief period of power Morgan greatly strengthened the defenses at Port Royal, since a French fleet was known to be roving around the Caribbean. The immediate danger to Jamaica ended when the French ships under Admiral d'Estrées ran aground on a small island called Aves.

An important part of the Earl of Carlisle's mission was to curb the House of Assembly in Jamaica, which was unruly and independent. To the English mind, this Assembly had several faults. It refused to mention the King's name in revenue bills, holding that the right to impose taxes was the Assembly's, not the King's. It also refused to vote any revenue bill for a period longer than two years, knowing that if a governor were assured of income he would not bother to call the Assembly into session.

Carlisle, who believed that the best way to rule was as an autocrat, arrived at Port Royal in almost regal splendor in July, 1678. He carried with him forty laws framed in London. These were to supersede the laws already on the books in Jamaica and to be the basis of a Jamaican constitution. Carlisle called a session of the Assembly in September and made a speech. He mentioned that the King thought of Jamaica as "his darling plantation." Then he presented the new laws for them to pass and with them a suggestion that the Assembly vote revenues that would be perpetual, not for just two years. He was asking, in effect, that it should vote itself out of power, an extraordinary suggestion to make to any politicians.

The Assembly, naturally, resisted the new Governor. One by one it voted down thirty-six of the forty measures he had brought with him. In a formal address to Carlisle it wrote, "Nor can we believe that his Majesty would have made this alteration had he been truly informed of his own interests." A good law could not be written in London to solve a problem of Jamaica, "which at a great distance is impossible to be known, being always distinguished with the false colors of interest and design."

Carlisle replied, "You are very dogmatical in your opinions." Then to a friend in England he complained, "Popular discourses prevail here as in England." After a month's session he dismissed the Assembly, having been able to get a revenue bill passed for only one year.

Out of Carlisle's forty laws, the one that had angered the As-

sembly most was one that proposed a change in voting proce-
dures. It had been the practice in Jamaica to pass a law, then send
it to the King for approval. The law remained in effect until he
disapproved. Under Carlisle's method, a proposed law would be
drafted, sent to the King to be studied and perhaps rewritten, and
then sent back to Jamaica to be voted on. Since a voyage between
the two lands took months, this did not seem very practical to the
Jamaicans.

The discussion between Carlisle and prominent Jamaicans
about the proposed changes in government went on in a courteous manner but not in a formal session of the Assembly. The
colonists complained that their right to debate was being taken
from them and that the proposed laws were too rigid to be of use
because "the nature of all colonies is changeable." They said that
the King must have been misled by his advisers, because what was
actually being proposed was a form of absolute government.

Carlisle passed these thoughts on to the government in London
and received an indignant reply. The colonies never had any *right*
to assemblies; these were merely a favor from the King, who had
permitted them only as an experiment. The King had not resigned
his power and given it to colonial legislators. If the government
should yield at all to the Jamaicans, what would be the effect on
other colonies? Carlisle must present the same laws to another
Assembly.

Meanwhile, Carlisle was beginning to see the Jamaican point of
view. He now wrote of the island's *grievances*. He called an Assembly and told the members he would send the Lieutenant Governor to England to negotiate a return to the old system. If he
failed, Carlisle himself would go to see what he might do. The
grateful Assembly voted a new revenue bill, to be good for six
months. Writing to London about this meeting, Carlisle said that
Jamaicans would never accept the new laws or "make chains for
their posterity." The same attitudes and arguments were the seeds
of the American Revolution.

Deliberations over the laws lasted for several years. In London former governors of Jamaica were asked their opinion of the crisis and of the rights of the colonists. The Chief Justice was also asked about the colonists' rights, and he concluded that they, "as Englishmen, ought not to be bound by any laws to which they had not given their consent." The government concluded that it could not win the battle with Jamaica. It would allow the Assembly to operate as before but, to save face, the government must have a permanent revenue bill, or at least one that would run for seven years.

In May, 1680, when deliberations were just begun, Carlisle returned to England to press the Jamaican point of view, as he had promised the Assembly he would do. He named Sir Henry Morgan acting governor in his absence.

Surprisingly, Morgan began to wage an active campaign against privateers soon after his return to power as lieutenant governor. He wrote to London, complaining about pirates from Santo Domingo and privateers from Jamaica who were luring white indentured servants away, and asked for small fast frigates which could pursue them into the small creeks where the King's large ships could not sail. He captured a particularly infamous pirate named Everson and reported proudly, "Such is the encouragement which privateers receive from my favor." On another occasion, again asking for ships, he reported that four cargoes of slaves had been smuggled ashore in fourteen days while His Majesty's frigate was at sea. "Privateers in the West Indies can be no less easily extirpated than robbers on the King's highway in England."

Morgan is a difficult man to understand. The man who sacked and destroyed Panama could also write, after the trial of some pirates, "I abhor bloodshed and I am greatly dissatisfied that in my short government I have been so often compelled to punish criminals with death."

After holding the Assembly in session for seven months, Morgan finally obtained a revenue bill that would last for seven years. He wrote to London that this great victory showed that he was a very hard-working servant of the Crown. But, he continued, though the Assembly granted the revenue, its members also granted themselves a few favors. They passed a law saying that all the laws of England were in force in the island, a subtle point questioned by the London authorities. Other bills secured their own personal liberties and properties. They stated that all money raised in taxes must be spent in Jamaica. They arranged matters so that the Assembly had to meet at least once a year. They added that no governor could force a Jamaican into military service. The King would have to put the final approval on all this, but, Morgan declared, if any major changes were made, another revenue bill would be almost impossible to get.

Morgan said that this long session of the Assembly had cost him a thousand pounds. "Governors at such a time are forced to keep open house."

While Sir Henry was performing this task, a letter was on its way revoking his commission. The Earl of Carlisle was heartily sick of the problems of Jamaica and had resigned as governor. Sir Thomas Lynch, who had been accused by Morgan and others of cheating and stealing, was reappointed governor.

VII

Days of Prosperity

When Sir Thomas Lynch returned to Jamaica in 1682 the English colony was only twenty-seven years old, but it was no longer in much danger of extinction. Now more than 100,000 acres were being planted by a slave force estimated at about fifty thousand that had been brought in since the end of the Dutch wars ten years before. Business was good and Port Royal continued to prosper by means of its brisk trade with privateers. Though Port Royal was rich, Sir Thomas found that the King's House there, as well as the one in Spanish Town he had complained about earlier, was in such bad repair that he stayed with his friend Colonel Molesworth, who commanded a regiment in Port Royal.

Lynch managed to get from the boisterous Assembly a new twenty-one-year revenue act, which he promptly forwarded to

London. It arrived while the lords were still sputtering over the report Morgan had transmitted about the last Assembly. The English government might have begun some drastic action against Jamaica for these acts, but the evidence that the Assembly seemed willing to cooperate with Lynch calmed the ministers down. They confirmed most of the acts sent by Morgan, but still urged Lynch to get a perpetual revenue. Lynch tried, telling the Assembly, "Princes cannot be bound, therefore they must be trusted." While this seemed less than impressive to the members of the Assembly, they did vote a revenue that extended for twenty-one years, and the English government, in return, extended the Assembly's last group of acts as confirmed for the same twenty-one years.

Lynch faced the same problems about the seas around his island that had troubled other governors. He asked London whether French buccaneers were legal agents of the French King or were instead to be treated as pirates. (Lynch received no reply. England did not want to annoy France.) What should he do about the Spanish? In Spain itself, the government was very weak. The King was a very sick infant who might not live long enough to produce any heirs. The country was ruled by a regency. Spain's government in the West Indies was almost as weak, but the English wanted the Spanish to stay there, as a buffer against the increasingly ambitious French. Therefore Spain must not be offended.

To a governor of Jamaica, however, the Spanish were a menace, despite their internal political weaknesses. They continued to attack Jamaican ships, seizing not only logwood but also cocoa, sugar, indigo, ginger and other produce from the West Indies, as if the Caribbean were still the Spanish Main. Lynch estimated that his island had lost about £25,000 worth of goods to Spanish marauders in the previous ten years. Three hundred English logwood cutters were being held prisoner.

Trying to keep the peace, Lynch ordered that there be no more sailing to Campeche and the logwood country in Mexico, but

privateers went there anyway. Spanish ships increased their po-
licing of the seas, and Lynch wrote a sharp letter to the Governor
of Havana, protesting the seizure, torture and murder of honest
merchants. He almost threatened war. He also sent a letter to the
Governor of Cartagena, taunting him with the Spanish failure to
deal with what they called pirates while preying in a cowardly
fashion on peaceful trade. Lynch's threats could be only idle
ones, however. Instructions to governors about starting wars had
become very strict since the days of Sir Thomas Modyford.

Lynch soon found that true piracy had increased in the Caribbean. This was not the kind of buccaneering activity authorized
in recent years by the French in Tortuga nor the privateering
commissioned from Port Royal, but marauding by men who had
no allegiance. Englishmen now captured not only Spanish ships
but French, Dutch and even English ones. Lawlessness of this
kind was not entirely new to the Caribbean, but Lynch found
that it had inceased dramatically.* The Governor had a number
of small sloops built, and one fifty-oar galley, to patrol the waters
around Jamaica. He reported to London that patrolling had been
successful, saying that he had not recently heard of a pirate from
Puerto Rico to the Gulf of Mexico. The government congratu-
lated him and then asked by what right was he commissioning
ships? The ministers asked the question of themselves too and,
deciding that the matter was unclear, gave Lynch's successor the
specific right to seize and try pirates.

Sir Thomas Lynch and Sir Henry Morgan had known each
other for ten years, beginning with Lynch's arrival in Port Royal
the first time, when he had had orders to arrest Morgan and send
him to England. Lynch had liked Morgan at first and had not sent
him back until Morgan recovered from an illness. Then, when
Morgan returned in triumph three years later, as lieutenant gov-

---

*Piracy continued to flourish in the area for the next fifty years. Blackbeard and
Captain Kidd both were active after the time of Henry Morgan. Blackbeard
was hanged on the Port Royal peninsula.

ernor, he had immediately removed Lynch and accused Lynch, who had returned to England, of illegal behavior, but the charges were never proved.

Coming back to Port Royal after an absence of seven years, Lynch found Morgan in possession of considerable power as lieutenant governor, judge of the Admiralty Court, and customs collector for Port Royal. Morgan was holding high commissions in both the Army and the Navy. And he was wealthy, from his days of privateering and from the success of the several plantations he owned.

Perhaps in defense against Morgan's power, Lynch wrote to England: "I greatly desire a dormant commission for Colonel Molesworth. Believe me, he is an intelligent, loyal virtuous gentleman who will serve the King and country. I will pawn my credit and life on it." Somewhat later he said, "In case of my death the island runs a great risk, for it will be ravaged. A blank commission would retrieve it." Some months later he wrote, "I must thank you sincerely for Colonel Molesworth's commission, for it is certain that Sir Henry Morgan's hope of governing as first Councillor has buoyed up his little senseless [political] party and occasioned its insolence and our late troubles. This you have now obviated. . . ."

Later in that year of 1683 Colonel Robert Byndloss, Morgan's brother-in-law, was expelled from the Council for striking Thomas Martin and using provoking language toward Colonel Molesworth.

A few days after this the Council met to hear Governor Lynch read a list of charges against Sir Henry Morgan. He was accused of having caused disorders in Port Royal and leading "ill" people to disturb the peace, of having on all occasions shown his dislike of the Governor, of creating a party against the revenue bill to spite the Governor, and of other extravagances.

Sir Henry replied only that he should not be blamed for the faults of others. He had often scolded others for misbehavior and he never intended to offend the Governor, so it was all up to the Governor. Sir Henry then walked out of the meeting.

A vote was taken and Sir Henry Morgan was removed from all his offices and commands. In an amendment to the official notice, a remark was made about a witness named Mrs. Wellen who had been called. She said she had heard Sir Henry go by her door one night, with others she did not know, and heard Sir Henry swear, "God damn the Assembly." The Governor said that others had heard Sir Henry make many strong expressions while in his wine.

Morgan and Byndloss sent a plea to the King to have him over-rule this dismissal, but His Majesty found in favor of Lynch.

The following summer Lynch died from one of the Jamaica fevers and his friend Molesworth was sworn in as governor almost immediately by the Council. No explanation was given for the haste in the matter, but perhaps the Council feared that Morgan would challenge the new Governor's commission.

During his time in office Molesworth had other troubles as well as those caused by Morgan and his friends. Privateers and pirates were attacking Jamaican fishermen hunting for turtles in the cays south of Cuba. Turtles were part of the daily diet for the several thousand people living at Port Royal, and turtle meat was also sent inland to Spanish Town and the plantations.

In connection with this, Molesworth wrote to the Governor of the town of Trinidad in Cuba:

> No sooner had I entered upon this Government on the death of Sir Thomas Lynch, when I received many complaints from honest traders and fishermen of injuries received from your nation, who treat them without any distinction as pirates and robbers. Among others, Derek Cornelison, with his sloop belonging to this harbour, was attacked without any warning by Don Juan Balosa, while peaceably trading on your coast, and taken into port where his sloop and goods were condemned, to the value of £6,000, his men

kept prisoners, and himself threatened with death till he was forced to fly to save his life. The pretence was that he was lieutenant of a galley sent hence by the late Governor for suppression of pirates. It is well for you that he escaped, or the whole town of Trinidad would have been too poor a satisfaction for such a violation of the law of nations. We have the same law as you against trading with foreigners but we do not treat your ships as you treat our sloops. If we suffer your ships to trade we protect them afterwards, and if not we give them fair notice to be gone. You permit the sloops to trade for a little to be the more sure of seizing them.

In a message to London, Molesworth reported: "A gentleman of quality in Cuba has given information that they design an invasion of the north side of this island, in the hope of getting Negroes. It is not unlikely and I have instructed the officers in that quarter to be very vigilant." Concerning some of the troublemakers he wrote:

> These galleys and pirogues are mostly manned by Greeks, but they are of all nations, rogues culled out for the villainies that they commit. They never hail a ship...They lurk in the bushes by the shore so that they see every passing vessel without being seen. When our sloops are at anchor they set them by their compasses in the daytime, and steal on them by night with so little noise that they are aboard before they are discovered. The Greek who was captain of a Spanish vessel, and who was condemned for piracy in Sir T. Lynch's time but reprieved, has since been accused of further piratical acts. I have set the law in motion and he will be executed on the 17th.

What trade existed between the Spanish and the English was mostly in slaves. Governor Molesworth was in the business himself. He wrote, "The Spaniard in this port has got but 150 Negroes for both his ships . . . When the great ship that is supposed to have fallen to leeward arrives, there will be freight enough for 1,500

Negroes and money to pay for them. Besides these another ship is expected from Cartagena that would carry 400 more." Then, noting that Port Royal did not have enough of the desired cargo, he remarked, "What precious opportunities are lost for want of Negroes!"

Molesworth had other concerns, too:

> One Gilbert, sometime chaplain of the *Guernsey*, was preferred by Sir Thomas Lynch to be rector of St. Dorothy's and should have had a very good livelihood. But having more of the beast than the man in him, he committed so many scandalous actions that he was rebuked by Sir Thomas Lynch. Remembering the rebuke but forgetting his preferment, he has published the most scandalous libel against Sir Thomas that ever was heard, unworthy of a Christian, much more one of his coat. He was indicted for this, fined £300, and imprisoned for twelve months, under which sentence he still lies.

Gilbert's libel was in the form of a poem. Some excerpts read:

> *He that would murder when he pleased*
> *And with the gout so oft diseased . . .*
> *Who made interest his only God*
> *Was for our sins the scourging rod . . .*
> *Who orphans cheated by his power*
> *Still seeking whom he might devour . . .*
> *Grew mad, and soon as madly died*
> *And now great ease Jamaica gains*
> *By his entering eternal pains . . .*

The poem does seem libelous, but perhaps Gilbert knew more about Lynch than has been recorded elsewhere.

On April 10, 1685, Jamaica received news of the death of Charles II, and the following morning, at Port Royal and Spanish Town, James II was proclaimed king "with all possible demonstrations of joy and satisfaction by all present." A few months later Molesworth learned that he was to be relieved by Sir Francis Howard, and then, Sir Francis having died, by the Duke of Albemarle. To Molesworth's consternation he then discovered that Sir Philip Howard's executors and the Duke of Albemarle were between them demanding three thousand pounds as governor's salary, though neither of the two had ever seen Jamaica. Molesworth complained that since he had been acting as governor he had been taking the whole governor's pay of two thousand pounds a year. What was more, he had spent it. "It is true that for a little time . . . we had a Spanish trade for Negroes, by which I made some advantage, though infinitely less than my enemies assert, but these profits came to me only as a merchant . . ." If he had to give up three thousand pounds, Molesworth said, he "had better not have been Governor."

Along with these troubles, Molesworth had to handle a serious slave rebellion. The members of the Assembly, all men of property and owners of slaves, were anxious to have the rebellion put down but did not wish to pay for it themselves. They proposed that the Government impose taxes on Negroes that were exported, a higher duty on wine, taxes on everything imported in foreign ships, and taxes on all money shipped out. Molesworth told the Assembly that he would not agree to any of this and that the King would never assent to such taxes "as [a means of] securing ourselves against our slaves." He proposed that the owners tax themselves, "to secure our estates by our estates," and added:

> I reckon that what is required of you [in property tax] does not exceed five shillings for every hundred pounds' value of our real estates. So if you intend to raise the money, set about it heartily. If not, tell me that I may know what to do. I have done my duty and if you fail to do yours the opposers of it will be answerable for any innocent blood that may be spilt on occasions that might have been prevented. I wash my hands of it.

This message to the Assembly did little good, so the angry Governor sent another:

> Your own minutes are sufficient to show . . . your own unsteady dealing. I shall only remind you that you have, all of you, acknowledged the necessity of raising the money required and voted that necessity unanimously, but have since been so cautious not to affect yourselves therewith that you have omitted nothing, however unreasonable, to ease yourselves therein, and would resolve upon nothing that would burden yourselves.
>
> You have been so fickle and inconstant that nothing was to be depended on from you. You have on several occasions voted one thing one day and contradicted it the next . . . Never was the venerable name of Assembly so dishonoured as at this time. All things have been carried on not by strength of argument or reason, but by noise and number of voices, led by malice and followed by ignorance. Since, therefore, your whole aim seems to be to take some little care of yourselves, but none of the poor people by whose labours and hazards you have so long slept in security, . . . I do in the King's name dissolve you, and you are hereby dissolved.

The Governor had a few satisfactions and pleasures, however. He was able to report that Captain Spragge had returned to Port Royal with Captain Banister, a notorious pirate, as his prisoner. Three of Spragge's men were now hanging at the yardarm. This was "a spectacle to all good people and of terror to the favourers of pirates, the manner of his punishment being that which will most discourage others, which was the reason I empowered Captain Spragge to inflict it. One of Banister's men was shot dead for refusing to surrender and two boys who were with him, under compulsion it seems, I have pardoned."

In another report he said, "Piracy has never received such checks as I have given it in the last few months nor have we ever been so free as lately from such vermin."

For pleasure there were celebrations at such times as the new King's birthday. A report to London said:

> The Governor reviewed the regiment, many of whom were in scarlet, which they had provided expressly for the day. The Governor entertained all the principal gentlemen and officers with a very sumptuous dinner; and in the evening the Governor's lady, being waited on by all the gentlewomen of quality, gave them a very fine treat, and afterwards entertained them at a ball, composed of a suitable number of masqueraders, very curiously habited, and variety of music, all managed with that admirable order as gave great beauty and grace to it. They continued dancing very late, but the streets shone with bonfires to light them home.

Port Royal was a town of remarkable contrasts: drunkenness and brawling in the streets, women of loose morals for the sailors, the public spectacle of pirates hanging from the yardarm, slave insurrections, the dishonorable Assembly, fevers, violent death on the high seas, and then this elegant governor's ball where all the people of "quality" gathered to dance in honor of the King.

The task of being governor of Jamaica was seldom easy. When Molesworth's successor, the Duke of Albemarle, arrived, one of the first things he did was to demand that Molesworth put up £100,000 in security for the King's share of the booty before he would be allowed to sail to England.

VIII

An Observant Chronicler Arrives

The Duke of Albemarle who came to Jamaica in 1687 was the second man to bear that title. His father, George Monk, had won fame as Cromwell's best general and had then arranged the restoration of Charles II. In reward the new King had elevated Monk to the peerage. Sir Thomas Modyford was Monk's cousin, and Monk had protected him at court until his death in 1670. It was in the year following Monk's death that Modyford was arrested and brought to London, where he must have sought out his cousin's son. The new Duke was not yet of age at the time, but he had already married the daughter of the Duke of Newcastle, entertained the King in the great house given him by his father-in-law, and also fought in Holland at the head of his own regiment. For all his youth, he could be a powerful friend. When Henry Morgan came as a prisoner to England some months after

Modyford, he too no doubt met Albemarle. This must have been so, because before he accepted his commission to Jamaica the Duke insisted that he be given power to reinstate Morgan and his relative Byndloss to the Council.

When Albemarle's appointment as governor of Jamaica was announced in England, his friends were amazed. He had the titles of Privy Councillor, Lord Lieutenant of two counties, Lord of Trade and Plantations, Captain of His Majesty's Life Guards, Chancellor of the University of Cambridge, and several other high offices. Why should he throw himself away on such a distant and rambunctious colony?

The answer was quite simply that he had been a very extravagant youth and needed money. He had already had to sell some of his property to support his lavish entertaining. From Jamaica he believed he could better exploit a fine new source of income, the wreck of a Spanish galleon.

Several years before, a Captain William Phipps, a New England carpenter with a reputation for discovering treasure, had been sent out in the *Algier Rose,* a frigate of the Royal Navy, to seek a Spanish cargo believed to have been lost in the Bahamas. On reaching the Caribbean, Phipps discovered that some of his crew were planning to seize the ship and become pirates. He took his ship to Port Royal and discharged the plotters, signing on a new crew. (This angered Governor Molesworth, who lost much-needed good men and gained more criminals. Of the latter, the Governor already had an oversupply.) Touching at the north shore of Santo Domingo, Phipps learned of a different Spanish treasure ship, one that had been lost on a reef. He had his men dive down and search for it, but finally he had to give up and return to England when his crew showed too much restlessness.

Phipps received no more support from the Royal Navy, but he did at last manage to interest the Duke of Albemarle in forming a group called the "Gentlemen Adventurers" that would finance a new expedition. Phipps returned to the supposed spot and, after many dives by Indians who were skilled in this work, the wreck was found. The amount of the prize was sensational. Phipps's divers kept bringing up wealth until he finally had to depart for lack of provisions to feed his crew. He was certain that much more of value lay on the sea bottom. Albemarle's share of what Phipps brought back amounted to £40,000. The Duke was anxious to secure more from the same source. (The total take was about £200,000 worth of silver, pearls and precious stones. Phipps's share was less than £10,000, but he was knighted and named governor of Massachusetts. Albemarle gave the new Lady Phipps a cup worth almost £1,000.)

The Duke was commissioned early in 1686 to govern Jamaica, but he did not leave for his post until the following September. Meanwhile, he consented to receive half pay. Beyond the usual powers of office, he was given full rights over any gold, silver or other mines found in America, the power to confer knighthood, the unusual right to return home without leave, and permission to reinstate Sir Henry Morgan to the Council.

The ducal party that sailed from Spithead on September 12, 1687, was a grand one. There were five hundred tons of baggage, one hundred servants, a chaplain, a secretary, the Duke and his Duchess, who was on the verge of insanity. To care for her the Duke brought along a brilliant young physician, Dr. Hans Sloane. The large group sailed in a convoy consisting of the *Assistance* (a Royal Navy frigate), two merchant ships, and the Duke's yacht, in the charge of his natural son, Captain Monk. Since the Duke himself was only thirty-five years old at the time, this Captain Monk cannot have been much more than a boy.

Dr. Sloane made interesting notes describing the three-month voyage. He was on board the *Assistance*, a ship with forty guns and two hundred men. The weather was rough and many people became seasick. Always a scientist, the doctor wondered what caused this effect, but was unable to find an answer. Because of the adverse wind, it took them twenty-two days to get out of the

English Channel. Then they found good weather and had a glorious sail southward. Sloane saw many whales and watched the sailors shoot porpoises, which they ate to supplement the wretched food served on the ship. The doctor also noted the phosphorescence of the ship's wake at night and speculated on its cause.

The captain wanted to get water and provisions at the island of Madeira and, not being able to find it, asked directions from passing ships. When they reached the port, Sloane went ashore and found little to his liking except the Madeira wine. The Inquisition was operating at full force. Women never went out except to go to Mass. No one ever entertained at home. Every man carried a dagger. No one went out on the street at night. A Negro would murder for a piece of eight. The island had much cholera.

Sloane wrote that he was glad when they got back to sea. He observed the sailors catching sharks in these warm waters with great hooks and chains and salt pork for bait. There were many cases of heat rash, something he had never seen before. As they approached Barbados, he admired the flight of the man-of-war birds.

The Duke called at Barbados for news of work at the profitable wreck Phipps had discovered. Little more had been found there, so the convoy sailed on to Jamaica, arriving at Port Royal on December 20. The Duke and Duchess did not disembark for six days. The Council had asked the Assembly to join in a suitable reception for this great peer of the realm, but the sullen Assembly would not cooperate. Finally the Duke and Duchess landed and were entertained for three days at public expense by the Council. A welcoming address declared that the Duchess' presence conferred "an honour which the opulent Kingdoms of Mexico and Peru could never arrive at; and even Columbus' ghost must be appeased for all the indignities he endured of the Spaniards, could he but know that his beloved soil was hallowed by such footsteps."

Sir Henry Morgan was certainly a member of the welcoming

party. He had regained much of the popularity he had lost after being dismissed from his posts, and he also had hopes of preferment from Albemarle.

His relative Colonel Byndloss was not there, however. Byndloss had incurred the wrath of some influential citizens by accusing them of receiving slaves smuggled onto the island by a privateering ship, the *Hawk*. In reply, one of the men accused, Colonel Samuel Barry, wrote: "If Colonel Byndloss knew of any malpractice here, why did he not complain to the Governor here instead of sending home malicious letters? Had he given information when the ship was at Port Maria and the Captain at Sir Henry Morgan's house close by, feasting on a fat guinea goat, then the Government could have made some use of his services." Since the captain was Morgan's friend, the matter must have been embarrassing to Morgan. Things got no worse, however, because Colonel Byndloss very suddenly died. He was fifty years old, a good age in that country.

A month after Albemarle's arrival, the Duke reported an earthquake. It was "generally felt all over the island, but no great harm done that I can hear."

The cordial atmosphere of the three-day welcoming reception —somewhat bogus in any case, since the Assembly would not cooperate—did not last very long. There was the dispute between Albemarle and former Governor Molesworth over the question of £100,000 security. Molesworth had placed chests of plate and coin aboard the ship in which he was to sail to England on May 12. These chests contained what Molesworth thought was the King's share of the wealth taken from Phipps's wreck. Albemarle disputed the amount, had the chests seized and would not let Molesworth sail unless he put up £100,000 as security. The whole confusing matter was settled by the King, who ordered that Molesworth be let go. Upon arrival in England in October he was relieved of his bond.

Then, Albemarle had trouble with his Council almost immediately, because they believed he favored Sir Henry Morgan. Members failed to attend meetings when summoned, and once so few men appeared that the meeting had to be called off.

Albemarle called for the election of a new Assembly two months after his arrival and got as new members two friends of Morgan, Roger Elletson and Colonel Needham. Both were partisans of Henry Morgan and therefore potential strong backers for Albemarle. (Elletson had been disbarred from the practice of law at the time of Morgan's downfall.) This Assembly soon came into conflict with Albemarle. During a debate on horse racing a new member, John Towers, said, "The well-being of the people is the supreme law." Colonel Needham angrily declared that these were dangerous and treasonable words. The Assembly voted to back Towers, so Needham appealed to the Governor. The Assembly publicly reprimanded Needham for this action and voted him out. Then the Governor began a prosecution of Towers and saw that he was heavily fined. The Assembly protested such a dictatorial act, so the Governor promptly dismissed them.

A new election was called and held in such a manner that supporters of the Governor had a distinct advantage. Some legal electors were put in prison in order that they might not be able to vote. Soldiers, discharged seamen and indentured servants were taken to the polls to vote, even though such people were not property owners and therefore were unqualified to vote. Some of the men were even taken from parish to parish, voting in each place. These methods worked and the Governor's party scored a great success. Only twelve men from the previous Assembly were reelected.

On July 12 Sir Henry Morgan rejoined the Council after an absence of five years. A few days later the Assembly met, and Roger Elletson, who had been called "crafty and unscrupulous" by his enemies, was unanimously elected Speaker. Elletson then made a long address, criticizing all recent governors except for Morgan, to whom he gave extravagant praise. He did not neglect to flatter the present Governor. For his reward, Elletson was given the office of chief justice of Jamaica.

Meanwhile, between treating patients, Sir Hans Sloane was making the first scientific study of the island. Sloane had been advised by an eminent London physician named Sydenham that it would be better to drown himself in the pond in St. James's Park than go to Jamaica, but Sloane, in spite of the ill health of the people around him, found himself in good condition and full of curiosity.

Sloane was a great collector, and from his trips into the mountains he brought back eight hundred kinds of plants, most of them new species. He had a local minister, a Reverend Mr. Moore, who was a skilled amateur artist, draw pictures of his plant samples, and also of creatures from the sea.

Sloane wrote about sea creatures at some length. He described land crabs, sea urchins, albacore tuna and the sting ray. He said the Carib Indians used to tip their arrows with the poison from the ray's tail. He discussed swordfish and freshwater eels, both delicious. He explained that garfish are practically boneless and taste good if fried with butter. Barracuda could also be eaten, as well as porgies, rockfish, snappers, mullet, iguanas, ducks, and turtles from the Cayman Islands. The turtles were kept alive in ponds on the Palisadoes peninsula (the new name for the land where Port Royal stood). Sloane also described how natives caught a nineteen-foot alligator, using a live dog for bait. He spoke, too, of a privateer at Port Royal named Rockey who, for sport, would dive into the water and slash sharks' bellies with his stiletto.

The island contained plenty of cattle, most of them wild, but the meat corrupted in two or three hours after butchering, so this work was done before dawn and the market was over by seven in the morning. The meat was cooked almost immediately. Sloane thought that, in Jamaica, swine's flesh that had been smoked and local poultry were better eating.

Sloane wrote that while masters might use flour, dried peas and salted mackerel imported from New England and New York, white and black servants got three pounds of salted meat a week, plus cassava bread, yams and potatoes. Poor people and sailors ate a great deal of cassava bread, but it was almost tasteless. Plantains or bananas were their next most important food.

The beer was not good. Much chocolate was drunk, but it was oily. A "cool drink" was a mixture of molasses and water. The rum punch, made with rum, water, lime juice, sugar and nutmeg, was cheap and very strong. Poor people who drank too much of it would "fall off their horses and lie on the ground sometimes whole nights exposed to the injuries of the air." Rum punch could lead to "consumptions, dropsies, and apoplectic fits." Though Jamaica had many rivers and springs, the well water at Port Royal was brackish and sailors who drank it often got "fluxes" (dysentery). Perhaps that was why they drank so much rum.

Sloane described the great fans found in some parlors. Presumably their motor power was slaves. He thought that the hammock most people slept in, due to the heat, were an excellent idea. He also approved of mosquito nets and thought it was a good idea that most people went to bed early and got up early.

Interested in just about everything, Sloane described how slaves were punished. For rebellion, the punishment was burning. The slave was nailed to the ground with crooked sticks to hold each limb. Then fire was applied by degrees to the hands and feet, then gradually to the head. Sloane wrote, "The pains are extravagant."

For lesser crimes, a man might be gelded or half his foot might be chopped off with an axe. For running away, slaves might have iron rings of great weight placed around their ankles or their necks or spurs put in their mouths. For negligence the punishment was to be beaten with a lance until bloody. Some masters put pepper and salt on wounds to make them smart.

Dr. Sloane wrote that punishments were given frequently.

He noted that slaves had come from all parts of western Africa and spoke many different languages and dialects. Those born in the West Indies were the most highly regarded, because they were more easily trained. The genetic mixing of white and Negro had begun, and Sloane spoke of mulattoes, mustees and quadroons, names describing proportions of black and white. The work in the fields was long and hard. Domestic servants were usually better treated.

White indentured servants, who might serve for as long as nine years, were hardly better off. Some were volunteers, but most of them had been deported from England for civil or criminal offenses or for having the wrong religious beliefs. Some of these had been handled so cruelly that the Assembly had passed a bill to protect them.

The planters lived in "great houses," always built on the highest ground on their estate. No other buildings were near them, and the grounds were always cleared to the distance of a musket shot. The stone walls were thick, with small slits through which muskets could be fired in any direction in case of attack. The shutters on the windows were made of "bullet wood," from a local tree, and these also had small slits in them. In Sloane's time no one had glazed windows or plastered walls. The ceilings were high, for the circulation of air, and the partitions between rooms only six to eight feet high. The furniture was crude, but everyone of position had quantities of silver plate, usually of Spanish origin, that had been acquired from the privateers in Port Royal. The cellars were usually well stocked with various brandies, the local rum, and port and Madeira wine, which were sufficiently strong in alcohol to survive the Atlantic crossing. The general atmosphere was much more that of a medieval castle than the gracious living usually associated with plantation life. The Middle Ages, usually considered to have ended with Columbus' discoveries, were not so far past for these settlers from England, and changes in styles of living were still very slow. Then, too, the slaves were a constant danger.

Sir Henry Morgan owned one of these "great houses" on an

Queen of the Holy Rosary College
Mission San Jose, CA. 94538
LIBRARY

estate to which he gave the Welsh name of Llanrumney. Here he lived part of the year, entertaining in the grand manner and "drinking late into the night" with neighbors and friends like Byndloss and the Duke of Albemarle. For part of the year he occupied his house in Port Royal, and it was while living here, suffering from the effects of his high living, that he became one of Sir Hans Sloane's patients.

Sloane had ideas on how to keep healthy in the tropics. He wrote, "Exercises here are not many, because of the heat of the air, riding in the mornings is the most ordinary, which by its very moving . . . has a very great power in keeping a man in sound health, as well as recovering a man when sickly and ill." Since Sir Hans lived in Spanish Town and treated people who lived in Port Royal, fifteen miles away, he must have done a considerable amount of riding himself.

He also had thoughts about the violent, dangerous life in Jamaica and the common overindulgence in drink.

> The passions of the mind have a very great power on mankind here, especially hysterical women and hypochondriacal men. These cannot but have a great share in the cause of several diseases, some of the people here being in such circumstances, as not to be able, to live easily elsewhere: add to this that there are not wanting some, as everywhere else, who have been of bad livers, whereby their minds are disturbed, and their diseases, if not rendered mortal, yet much worse to cure than those who have sedate minds and clear consciences.

One of Sir Hans's patients was Mrs. Thomas Barrett, a lady who had married into the ever-growing family that arrived in Jamaica at the time of Penn and Venables. She lived in one of Port Royal's better houses, a three-story building of red brick, right on Wharfside Street. When Sloane was called in she had fallen into a "Tertian," or fever. She was delirious and her tongue was black. Her children and grandchildren were gathered around her. The doctor wrote, "She had by her several cordials, as Bolus's of Diascord, etc., by which I supposed had in part brought her to this." The preparation in question contained one tenth of a grain of opium, and Mrs. Barrett may have taken a good deal of it. Dr. Sloane did not criticize her previous physician, but he did take her off the drug. He put her on some cooling, diluting drinks and prescribed a medicine called Cortex Peru. He was happy to report that "she entirely recovered."

Sloane had become friends with Henry Morgan, and Morgan, an intelligent, observant man, had given the doctor-scientist much useful information. But, Albemarle reported to the government in London, "I have admitted Sir Henry Morgan to the Council pursuant to the King's order, but I am afraid that he will not live long, being extraordinarily ill."

Sir Hans wrote about Morgan's symptoms and the treatment he gave him. Sir Henry had become lean and sallow-colored, his eyes a little yellowish, and he had developed a prominent belly. He complained about his lack of appetite and a feeling of nausea every morning. In modern medical terms this sounds like cirrhosis of the liver, brought on by years of heavy drinking. Sir Hans prescribed a bitter tonic for Morgan to take every morning and advised him to abstain from alcohol. Morgan began to feel very well again and "not being able to abstain from company he sat up late drinking too much." His symptoms soon reappeared.

Sir Hans called in a colleague, a Dr. Rose, who agreed about the bitter tonic, and together he and Sloane suggested another prescription, oil of scorpion and opiates, for a cough Morgan had developed. For a time the patient improved.

Morgan seemed unable to change his habits, however, so he soon became ill again. Not willing to follow Sloane's temperance advice, he called in three or four other doctors, who tried various remedies that were not of much use since the basic problem was alcohol. Then Morgan tried a black doctor who had a reputation for the practice of African folk medicine. This man gave him an enema made of urine and some drugs and then plastered Morgan's body in wet clay. This only made his coughing worse. Morgan sent for still another doctor, who promised to cure him. But the patient languished, his cough became terrible, and he died soon after, on August 25, 1688, at the age of fifty-three. His case had probably been hopeless, but his physicians no doubt hastened the end.

A funeral service was held the following day at Christchurch in Port Royal, and then Sir Henry Morgan was laid to rest in the Palisadoes burial ground. All the forts of the town fired a salute, then the guns of the Royal Navy ships *Drake* and *Assistance* fired a twenty-two-gun salute, and this was followed by more salutes from all the merchant ships in the harbor. No matter how others may have judged him, Port Royal gave full honors to its most famous citizen.

Morgan's will reflects some of the atmosphere of his times and indicates how profitable the life of a privateer could be. All his real estate was left to his "very well and entirely beloved wife, Dame Mary Elizabeth Morgan." With all the records that still exist about Sir Henry's later life, this is one of the very few mentions of the lady. The three exceptions to this legacy suggest that Morgan owned a considerable amount of land. One estate, called Penkarne, was to go to Morgan, the minor son of his brother-in-law, Robert Byndloss. Another estate, called Arthur's Land, went to Richard Elletson, the son of Roger Elletson. The estate of Danks was to be sold to pay Sir Henry Morgan's debts. On Lady Morgan's death, which occurred eight years later, her lands were to go to her nieces and nephews of the Byndloss family, on condition that they take the name of Morgan and "always go thereby."

Sir Henry's friend Colonel Thomas Ballard was willed the "green saddle with the furniture thereto belonging." Sir Henry's sister, Catherine Lloyd, was to receive an annuity of sixty pounds a year to be "yearly paid into the hands of my ever honest cousin, Mr. Thomas Tredegar" in Wales. Ten working Negroes in good condition and two horses or mules were to go to Morgan Byndloss on his twenty-first birthday. The sum of one hundred pounds was left to the parish of St. Mary. Roger Elletson was to have the choice of any one of Sir Henry's horses, his blue saddle, and one case of pistols tipped with silver. Each of his godsons received a silver-hilted sword and a mourning ring. (Such rings, worn in memory of the deceased, were an English custom until modern times.) His servants all received small amounts of money, as well as mourning rings. Mourning rings were to be offered to the Duke and Duchess of Albemarle with "a most humble desire that they will be pleased to accept the same." Other such rings were to go to a long list of friends he enumerated and, if he had omitted any, Lady Morgan, who was the executor, should include them at her discretion.

Sir Hans Sloane soon had another critically ill patient on his hands. Even before he had sailed from England the Duke of Albemarle was suffering from "dropsy," a condition in which the body swells due to the retention of unusual amounts of water. Dropsy can result from a number of causes, but Sloane felt that the Duke's case was caused by his high living. Sloane worried that the heat of Jamaica would be too much for his employer and noted that, soon after he arrived, the Duke had given up riding and begun enjoying a sedentary life with much sitting up late and making merry with his friends. Sloane suggested a move to Liguanea, the site of the present Kingston, for a change in air. This helped very little and the Duke died in October, 1688, at the age of thirty-five. Since Sloane's mission had been to keep Albemarle alive, the doctor felt it necessary to write: "It is most unfair to be charged with lack of success in the treatment of a patient who refuses to accept your counsel and advice."

In that hot climate, the dead were buried almost immediately and embalming was unknown. The Duchess, however, insisted that the Duke's body be taken to England, so Sir Hans had to act as the embalmer. After removing the inner organs, the doctor preserved the remains in pitch and encased them in a coffin within a coffin. The removed parts were buried below the altar of the church in Spanish Town.

A few weeks after Albemarle's death, England had a revolution—though, of course, Jamaica did not know it for months. James II had managed to make himself detested by almost everyone in the country. His elder daughter had married the Dutch Prince William of Orange, and the two of them were invited by Parliament to take over the government. King James could find so few supporters when William and Mary landed that he had to flee to France.

In Jamaica, in the absence of a governor, Sir Francis Watson, President of the Council, acted in that capacity, while the increasingly strange Duchess continued to live for a time in the King's House. She had the Duke's treasure, his furniture and his servants, but little protection. The ducal yacht, under the Duke's son, Captain Monk, was in Boston for repairs. For a time it seemed that Sir Hans Sloane was her only protector, but then the Assembly voted a bill in favor of "the disconsolate Princess" and sent militia to guard her when she moved to the country for a time. The widow had a great deal of wealth about her and in those rough times there were many who would be willing to take it away, by violence if necessary.

It took six months before all matters could be readied for her return home with her treasure, her furniture, her servants, and the Duke's coffin. With Sloane as her guardian, she boarded the Royal Navy's *Assistance* at Port Royal in the middle of the night. The next morning the frigate sailed, along with the now returned yacht and thirteen merchant ships.

When the party left Jamaica, they knew that James II was no longer king, but they did not know who reigned in his place. The captain of the *Assistance* said that if the King was in exile he would sail to France and put the ship at his disposal. The frightened Duchess, with all her possessions, her people and her husband's body, grew terrified at the thought of landing helpless on foreign soil. She begged the captain to change his mind, but that loyal Stuart follower would not.

Dr. Sloane wrote, "On hearing this assurance, the Duchess resolved on desperate measures." In the middle of the ocean, she, with all her valuables, her people, the Duke's coffin and Dr. Sloane, transferred to the Albemarle yacht. Then, finding this far too small, they all transferred again in the middle of a storm to the merchant ship *Generous Hannah*. Finally arriving at Plymouth, England, after a voyage of two and a half months, they found the *Assistance* peacefully anchored. The captain had changed his mind and sworn allegiance to the new King William.

Four years later the Duchess married the Earl of Montague, thinking he was the Emperor of China. On his death she was judged legally insane.

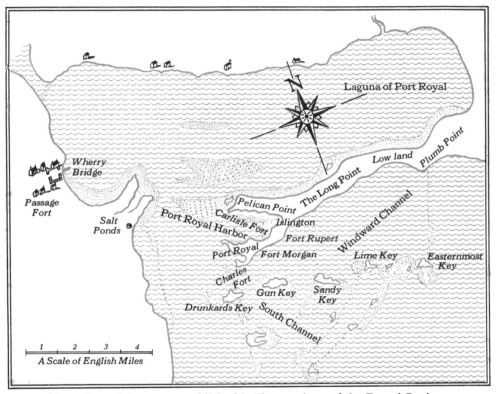

Map adapted from one published in Transactions of the Royal Society
in 1694, to accompany the descriptions contributed by Sir Hans Sloane

The End of Port Royal

As the year 1692 began, the weather along the south coast of Jamaica was unusually hot and dry and the air very still. From Port Royal, the tops of the high Blue Mountain Range across the bay, generally covered with clouds, could be seen with remarkable clarity. The extraordinary heat continued for months, while the people sweltered. Ordinary seamen, drinking, wenching, roistering in the streets, dressed for the climate: they wore only a loose shirt and a pair of breeches that stopped at the knee. The Negroes who slaved at loading and discharging ships wore even less.

The people with the social pretensions and the power, however, those who owned the fine brick houses along Wharfside Street (Henry Morgan's was among them), affected to appear in public as they would on the streets of London, in the richest possible clothes. Men of this class wore beaver hats with the brim turned up on one side, in the Cavalier style, and their long hair hung down to their shoulders. The lace cuffs of their shirts were so long that they concealed their hands.

A formal portrait of one of the richest planters, Colonel Peter Beckford, shows him at an open window with Fort Charles, at Port Royal, in the background. He is wearing a coat, heavily embroidered in gold, that hangs to his knees. The coat is scarlet and is made out of either wool or velvet. His long stockings are thick and white. He carries a sword, and his enormous hat with ostrich feathers rests on the windowsill. This was Beckford's finest outfit, no doubt, and one he would wear on important occasions, no matter what the weather.

The ladies of quality were hardly less elegant. They piled their hair high over their heads and decorated the constructions with ribbons and jewels. A lady might admire the value of the fabric of another's dress much more than its convenience. The extravagant costumes of the time were, in part, a revolt against the short-lived Puritan regime and, in part, a display to show a person's worth. This mattered more than comfort.

The place to live in overcrowded Port Royal was as close to the water as possible. This meant right next to the docks where the privateers and the slave ships landed. Real estate in the town was as expensive as in the center of London. This dockside land was valued because it provided a view better than the mean, narrow and unpaved streets, because there was a better chance of getting a breath of fresh sea air, and because it was close to the owners' places of business.

Business at Port Royal in 1692 was flourishing, no matter what the weather. Sugar was becoming the major export, but there was still a brisk, illicit trade with Spanish ports in the West Indies and with men who, since the Crown no longer commissioned them, must be called pirates. There was also the perfectly legal trade in slaves. The gentry who lived by the docks—churchgoers and law-abiding men when it suited them—could not avoid seeing the arrival of the slave ships. To most people today, watching the discharge of these terrified, bewildered Africans would provoke emotions of pity and horror. The poor slaves had been months crossing the Atlantic, shackled, starved, kept below decks in hot and fetid quarters that killed all but the most robust. A slave ship might throw as much as half its cargo, dead, overboard to the sharks. No one, it seems, among the lords of Port Royal had any emotions about the matter during the town's last days of glory. These Africans were commodities, not people, and an important source of the gold which built the proud houses. (The very word "guinea," still a value in English currency, derives from the Guinea coast from where the slaves were shipped.) Watching a slave ship disembark was not an emotional experience but a sport.

Behind the dock area, man-made with pilings and filling, lay a town of about two thousand houses. The population was about 3,500 people, larger than New York's at the time. Cramped, unhealthy and wanton, this frontier town was settled mainly for reasons of lust or greed. Yet a few men of honor lived there, among them the Reverend Dr. Emmanuel Heath of Christchurch and Sir Hans Sloane, who had returned to Jamaica with his wife and children after delivering the benighted Duchess of Albemarle to England.

The strange weather that had plagued Port Royal since January in 1692 changed in May to a siege of rain and high winds. This continued throughout the month, and then in June conditions again became very hot, still and dry.

On the morning of June 7 Dr. Sloane and his son set out for the mainland by canoe to visit some patients in Spanish Town. They had to paddle because there was not enough wind for a sail. In Port Royal, Dr. Heath attended divine service as he did every morning, hoping to set an example for "a most ungodly, debauched people." Dr. Heath was due for lunch at the house of Captain Ruden, but he stopped first at an inn to have a glass of wormwood wine with a merchant friend "to whet the appetite." Dr. Heath waited impatiently while his friend very slowly finished smoking his clay pipe. The reverend was a courteous man and did not want to be late for his engagement. Then, at twenty minutes before noon, while still at the inn, he felt the earth begin to heave and roll beneath him. "Lord, Sir," he shouted, "what is this?"

His friend replied, "It is an earthquake. Be not afraid. It will soon be over."

Dr. Heath ran into the street and, within moments, felt two much greater shocks. By the time he arrived at Captain Ruden's house, the building itself had vanished into the sea, along with three or four blocks behind Wharfside Street. In panic Dr. Heath raced toward Morgan's Fort, only to see it crumbling. Then before his eyes his church and its high tower fell. He saw the earth open up and swallow people. The sea began mounting behind him as he hurried toward his own home. It was still intact. He could think of nothing to do but kneel down in the street and pray. Many neighbors came to join him and, to his astonishment, a number of Jews from Jew Street. "They were heard to call upon Jesus Christ," he later reported.

During the same moments a frigate called the *Swan* broke its moorings and plunged inland over the sinking houses. The ship crushed one house, then rested on top of another without capsizing.

A French Huguenot refugee named Lewis Galdy was sucked out to sea by the first great seismic wave, then miraculously returned to land by the second.

A young Mrs. Akers was swallowed up in a gap in the land, then somehow ejected, and within three minutes she was rescued by a ship. Many others, similarly caught, were crushed to death in the earth's viselike grip. Colonel Beckford was saved from this fate by one of his Negro slaves, who shoveled him out.

Many people lay in the streets that had not yet flooded, killed by stones from falling buildings.

Sir Henry Morgan's grave was obliterated, along with the church.

Sir Hans Sloane and his son were in the middle of the bay when the earthquake struck. Sloane wrote:

> We were near being overwhelmed by a swift rolling sea, six feet above the surface, without any wind; but it pleased God to save us, being forced back to Linguanea, where I found all houses even with the ground; not a place to put one's head in, but in Negro houses. The terrible earthquake shook down and drowned nine-tenths of the town of Port Royal in two minutes time, and all by the wharfside in less than one. Very few escaped there. I lost all my people and goods, my wife and two men, Mrs. B. and her daughter. One white maid escaped who gave me an account that her mistress was in her closet, two pair of stairs high, and she was sent into the garret, where Mrs. B and her daughter were, when she felt the earth quake and bid her take up her child and run down, but, turning about, met the water at the top of the garret stairs, for the house sunk right down and is now under thirty feet of water.

The earthquake sank the narrow sandbar that connected Port Royal to the mainland and made it an island again. It destroyed all the houses in Spanish Town except those built before the English conquest. Most of the planters' houses in the countryside were destroyed. On the north shore of Jamaica more than a thousand acres of land were submerged. One mountain fell and completely covered a whole plantation. Other mountains moved considerable distances.

Several hundred people found safety on the *Swan*, the ship that had been washed ashore. Others managed to get to the solid ground on which the remaining one of three forts had been built. Still others, like Dr. Heath, managed to get to ships in the harbor that had been able to ride out the wild seas. From the *Granada*, Dr. Heath wrote a letter about the destruction of "Port Royal, the fairest town of all the English plantations, the best emporium and mart in this part of the world, exceeding in its riches, plentiful in all things." He called the event "the terrible judgement of God."

The aftermath was almost worse than the event itself. The thieves and drunkards of the town, those who lived through the earthquake, were seen looting whatever houses remained and stripping corpses of their rings and other jewelry. The earth shocks opened graves, and cadavers were strewn about. Dr. Heath saw wild dogs eating corpses. The bay was filled with hundreds of other corpses. Each day more houses fell into the sea. Dr. Sloane wrote, "The earth continues to shake five or six times every twenty-four hours. Great parts of the mountain fell down and fall daily. I pray God divert those heavy judgements which still threaten us."

Another account, by an unnamed writer, says, "We have had a great mortality since the great earthquake (for we have little ones daily). Almost half the people that escaped from Port Royal are dead of a malignant fever, from change of air, want of dry houses, warm lodging, proper medicines, and other conveniences."

On top of everything else, as the Reverend Thomas Hardwicke wrote, "Our first fears were concerning our slaves, those irreconcilable enemies of ours, who are no otherwise our subjects than as the whip makes them, who seeing our strongest houses demolished, our arms broken, and hearing of the destruction of our greatest dependency, the town of Port Royal, might in hopes of liberty be stirred up to rise in rebellion against us."

The reverend's fears were quite reasonable. Many slaves did escape during all the disorder. They joined the Maroons in the mountainous cockpit country, where the English never succeeded in conquering them. In 1738, after forty years of fighting, the English had to sign a treaty of peace instead.

Epilogue

Anyone flying today to Kingston, Jamaica, will land at the Palisadoes Airport. The plane will almost certainly pass over the site of Port Royal, about two miles away. After the great earthquake Jamaicans founded the city of Kingston, but they planned to rebuild Port Royal too, until a fire in 1702 destroyed what remained after the original disaster.

Now only Fort Charles remains from the once vibrant town, and even it was thoroughly rebuilt during the time when Admiral Nelson commanded it. There is a church that was constructed in the area in 1825, and Lewis Galdy's gravestone is in its cemetery. Visitors will also be shown some silver plate and a tankard said to have been stolen from Panama and donated by Sir Henry Morgan. The rest of Port Royal now consists of a new marina, perhaps fifty houses, a police academy, and the ruins of a naval hospital that was built long after the earthquake.

For years divers have been going down into the water where the town submerged. Probably most of the lost treasure has long since been discovered, but a few years ago a watch was found that had stopped at seventeen minutes before twelve. This was the time of the third and greatest shock. Also discovered at this time were the remains of a kitchen. Lunch had obviously been being prepared and it would have featured a turtle-and-beef stew. Such relics, along with coins, pottery, glassware and other things that may still be found, are being shown in a new Port Royal museum.

But what can be learned from the wild story of this town that vanished? Did the Lord destroy it in his wrath? Perhaps, but He has destroyed many others as well with no such good claim for His retribution. Is the moral that men are simply foolish to build on such a location? Is there some kind of moral to be learned from the people who lived there, all the wicked, vain, brutal, quarrelsome, greedy, lecherous people and even the occasional good people? Can we congratulate ourselves on being so much better than they were? Maybe we are just a little bit more civilized than the people who once inhabited Port Royal. Perhaps, seeing their failings at a comfortable distance, we may be better able to understand our own.

BOOKS OF INTEREST

For readers interested in further literature on Port Royal or the island of Jamaica or the history of the period, the following books should be available in most public libraries.

CARGILL, MORRIS, ED., *Ian Fleming Introduces Jamaica.*
New York: Hawthorn Books, 1966.
HARMAN, CARTER, AND THE EDITORS OF *Life* MAGAZINE, *The West Indies.*
New York: Time, Inc., 1963.
LINK, MARIAN CLAYTON, "Exploring the Drowned City of Port Royal,"
National Geographic magazine, February, 1960.
MORISON, SAMUEL ELIOT, *The Oxford History of the American People.*
New York: Oxford University Press, 1965.
PEPYS, SAMUEL, *Diary.* There are many editions of this famous work.
The Modern Library publishes a condensed, one-volume edition.
PETERSON, MENDEL, *History under The Sea.*
Washington, D.C.: The Smithsonian Institution, 1965.
ROBERTS, W. ADOLPHE, *Jamaica: The Portrait of an Island.*
New York: Coward McCann, Inc., 1955.
STEINBECK, JOHN, *Cup of Gold.* Several editions of this romantic biography of Sir Henry Morgan have been published. Bantam Books has one available in paperback.
WAUGH, ALEC, *A Family of Islands.*
New York: Doubleday and Co., 1964.

Some libraries may have copies of the excellent periodical *Jamaica Historical Review.* The two most interesting sources of all are usually found only under lock and key in rare-book rooms. Edward Long's *The History of Jamaica* was published in London in 1774. Sir Hans Sloane's *A Voyage to Jamaica* (and other islands) appeared in London in 1707. Both fascinating books have been out of print ever since but are worth the trouble of inquiring to see if they may be looked at.

INDEX

A

Africa, 14, 43
Albemarle, Duchess of, 93
  husband's death, 105-107
Albemarle, Duke of, 90-107
  excesses and death of, 105-107
  rigs Jamaica election, 98
  youth and extravagance, 93
Alexander VI, Pope, 19
Arawak Indians, 17
Assembly, Jamaica House of, 48,
  49, 60, 79-83, 90, 96-98

B

Banister, Major General, 74
Barbados, 15, 20, 73, 96
  early prosperity, 24
  helps colonize Jamaica, 34, 42
  independent spirit of, 24-25,
  47
  Modyford leaves, 47-48
  and Henry Morgan, 59
  Sedgwick's visit, 32
Barrett family, 25
Beckford, Colonel Peter, 110, 112

Brayne, General, 34
Brethren of the Coast, 11, 60, 77
Buccaneers, 20, 22, 50, 54, 66
  as privateers, 34
  discover Port Royal, 38
  early history, 10-13
  Panama attack, 69-72
  town's only defense, 55
Byndloss, Colonel Robert, 60, 77,
  86, 97, 104

C

Cagua, 10, 36
Caguaya River, 26
Campeche, 45, 52, 76, 84
Carib Indians, 20
Caribbean, 14, 19, 20, 62
Carlisle, Earl of, 78-82
Cartagena, 65, 85
Catholic, 11, 20, 57
Cavaliers, 21
Chagres River, 70-71
Charles I, King, 12, 20, 24
Charles II, King, 24, 28, 43
  death of, 89
  restoration of, 39

119

ABOUT THE AUTHOR

Peter Briggs, who was born in St. Paul, Minnesota, is a graduate of the University of Chicago. During World War II he served as an officer in the U.S. Navy. He has lived in several European countries and traveled throughout the world. Before becoming a full-time writer, he worked as a magazine editor. He now makes his home in New York City.

Mr. Briggs's other books include *Mysteries of Our World: Unanswered Questions About the Continents, the Seas, the Atmosphere, the Origins of Life; Men in the Sea*, a collection of biographies about men prominent in oceanography; and *Science Ship: A Voyage Aboard the* Discoverer.